SEVEN SECRETS OF BIBLE-MADE MILLIONAIRES

SEVEN SECRETS OF BIBLE-MADE MILLIONAIRES

TOYE ADEMOLA

Unless otherwise indicated, Scripture quotations are from The New King James Version. Copyright © 1979, 1980, 1982, Thomas Nelson, Inc., Publishers.

Scripture quotations marked KJV are from the King James Version of the Bible.

Scripture quotations marked AMP are from The Amplified Bible: Old Testament. Copyright © 1962, 1964 by Zondervan Publishing House (used by permission); and from The Amplified New Testament. Copyright © 1958 by the Lockman Foundation (used by permission).

Scripture quotations marked TLB are from The Living Bible, copyright © 1971. Used by permission of Tyndale House Publishers, Inc., Wheaton, Illinois 60189. All rights reserved.

Take note that the name satan, related names, and references are not capitalized. We choose not to give him any respect, even to the point of violating grammatical rules.

Printed in Canada

Publishing services by Selah Publishing Group, LLC, Arizona. The views expressed or implied in this work do not necessarily reflect those of Selah Publishing Group.

ISBN 978-1-58930-173-3
Library of Congress Control Number: 2006909650

Contents

Part 1

God Wants You to Be Wealthy!

Let them shout for joy and be glad, Who favor my righteous cause; And let them say continually, "Let the LORD be magnified, Who has pleasure in the prosperity of His servant."

Psalm 35:27

Wealth Belongs to You!

> A good man leaves an inheritance to his children's children, But the wealth of the sinner is stored up for the righteous.
>
> Proverbs 13:22b

One of the devil's oldest lies is: Money is evil.

Through the years, he has deceived many precious saints into believing that it is wrong for a Christian to be wealthy. For this reason, many in the Body of Christ have steered away from money as if it were a contagious disease. They honestly think that the poorer you are, the easier it is for you to live a holy life. This is a lie from the very pit of hell!

Money, or the lack of it, has nothing to do with your *salvation* or *sanctification*. Your financial status has nothing to do with your standing with God. Only the shed blood of the Lord Jesus Christ is powerful enough to justify you before God. Money, in and of itself, can neither keep you pure nor defile you. You know very well that there are wicked poor people, just as there are wicked rich people. But there are also some very rich people who are upright and righteous before the Lord.

Job, who was described as one of the most righteous people to have lived under the Old Covenant, was also one of the wealthiest.

> There was a man in the land of Uz, whose name was Job; and that man was blameless and upright, and one who feared God and shunned evil. And seven sons and three daughters were born to him. Also, his possessions were seven thousand sheep, three thousand camels, five hundred yoke of oxen, five hundred female donkeys, and a very large household, so that this man was the greatest of all the people of the East.
>
> Job 1:1-3, emphasis mine

God never ever said that money is evil. He said that *the love of money* is the root of evil (1 Timothy 6:10). There is a big difference! It is the love of money, not money itself, that is evil. It is not wrong to have money, but *it is wrong for money to have you.* It is not evil to possess money; *it is evil for money to possess you.*

The truth is: Wealth, not poverty, is your portion as a believer. Does Proverbs 13:22 say that poverty is stored up for the righteous? No! It says that wealth is! Friend, make no mistake about it, wealth is your portion. You are the righteousness of God in Christ, and the Bible says there is wealth stored up for you. Your good God has given you a rich inheritance. Every treasure in the heavens above and the earth beneath belong to God. And as His heir, what belongs to Him also belongs to you!

God is the God of abundance. He is not an average God. He is a God of excellence and affluence. All the silver and gold in the world belongs to our God (Haggai 2:8). He owns the cattle on a thousand hills (Psalm 50:10). It is absurd to think that a God of immeasurable wealth would support poverty. Search the Scriptures from Genesis to Revelation, and you will discover that *poverty*, *mediocrity*, and *barrenness* are words that are never used in association with God. Never! If poverty or mediocrity can't be found with your Father, it has no business being in your camp.

Salvation in Christ is not a call to poverty. *It is a call to prosperity! Jesus said, "Assuredly, I say to you, there is no one who has left house or brothers or sisters or father or mother or wife or children or lands, for My sake and the gospel's, who shall not receive a hundredfold* ***now in this time****—houses and brothers and sisters and mothers and children and lands, with persecutions—and in the age to come, eternal life"* (Mark 10:29-30, emphasis mine).

Here you see it stated plainly by the Master Himself. Everyone, without exception, who has left all to follow Him will receive a hundredfold blessing, not just in the sweet by and by, but right here and now, during their time on the earth!

Yes, my friend, *God wants you to have wealth.*

When the Lord God brought the Israelites out of the land of Egypt, *He also brought them out with silver and gold, and there was none feeble among His tribes* (Psalm 105:37). Egypt represents life before salvation in Christ—a life of bondage to sin, poverty, sickness, and defeat. Christ came to deliver mankind not just from sin, but from every kind of evil, including poverty and mediocrity.

God did not create a poor world. He made a rich world, filling it with His abundant possessions. Psalm 104:24 says, *O LORD, how manifold are thy works! in wisdom hast thou made them all: the earth is full of thy riches* (KJV). God filled the earth with His riches because it is His will for the inhabitants of the earth to live blessed and prosperous lives.

Poverty is not part of God's plan for man. Sin is what brought poverty into the world. Hard labor, struggle, suffering, and fruitless toil are all the painful result of Adam's fall (Genesis 3:17-19). But the Lord Jesus rectified the situation. *Though He was [so very] rich, yet for your sakes He became [so very] poor, in order that by His poverty you might become enriched (abundantly supplied)*" (2 Corinthians 8:9, AMP).

Jesus, your Savior and Lord, became *so very poor* so that you may become *so very rich* ... abundantly supplied. There is no reason whatsoever why you should not prosper in all things. There is no reason why you should live from paycheck to paycheck. *Super abundance*, not *scarcity*, is your portion in life.

Poverty is evil. It is not of God. It is a tormenting thief that steals much more than your finances. It steals your dreams. It is one thing for you to have a plan or vision for your life, ministry, and family; it is another thing for you to accomplish it. No matter how great and grand the dream God births in your heart, without money it cannot see the light of day. Ecclesiastes 10:19 says, *Money answers everything.*

As anointed as our Lord's earthy ministry was, He needed money to carry out His mission. We know money was an important factor in His ministry because the Bible tells us that He had a treasurer, Judas, who kept the ministry's money box (John 12:6). He wouldn't have needed a treasurer or a money box if they were just counting pennies! He also had ministry partners who continually gave to Him of their substance to help Him accomplish His work (Luke 8:1-3).

Jesus' disciples lacked nothing. They were well provided for because He had more than enough money to cover their expenses, as well as to conduct great citywide meetings. If Jesus needed money to fulfill His work on earth, how much more will you and I? Make no mistake about this: You need money to realize your God-given visions.

There is absolutely nothing good about poverty. It takes away from a person. It does not add to him or her. Poverty robs you of the ability to bless those around you. God does not subtract from you. He multiplies you! He empowers you to fulfill your life's assignment. Beloved, do not doubt for one second that your Father wants you to be rich, not poor.

What kind of father would live in wealth while his offspring languished in lack and squalor? Why, then, would anyone think less of our Heavenly Father? How is it that anyone would consider earthly parents more benevolent and caring than God? To say that God wants His people to be poor is to call Him a name that He is not. God is not stingy. He is not irresponsible. NO! He is loving and kind. He is caring. He is good. And as a good Father, He has given His children a lavish inheritance. He has stored up wealth for them.

He is delighted (as any parent would be) when you are prospering. Psalm 35:27 says, He *has pleasure in the prosperity of His servant.* God has ordained that wealth and riches will be in the house of the righteous.

> The generation of the upright will be blessed. Wealth and riches will be in his house, And his righteousness endures forever.
>
> Psalm 112:2b-3

Are you the righteousness of God in Christ? Then say out loud, "Wealth and riches will be in my house!"

Wealth Means *Having More Than Enough*

You may say, "Well, I am not poor. I have a good salary. My family is well provided for. I even have some money saved up for a good retirement. Is this book really for me?" You bet it is!

The wealth I am talking about is the overflowing, never-ceasing, super-abundant provision of God. God does not only want you to have *just enough* or *a little more than enough.* He wants you to have *much more than enough*. He wants your cup of financial blessings to literally run over!

Wealth is the state of being rich and affluent; having a plentiful supply of material goods and money. This is how God wants you to live. God wants you to live a life of profuse abundance where all your needs are met *and* you have so much more left over! He wants you to live an above-average life, possessing a plentiful supply of material goods and money. He wants you to be out of debt, having all your needs met, with plenty left over to be a blessing to others!

God is the most benevolent Being. Whatever He gives, He gives in great quantity. He gives beyond measure. You need to have the right mentality about God. The way some Christians talk about God you would think He is so tight-fisted. In reality, He is extraordinarily open-handed. Psalm 145:16 says of our God, *You open Your hand and satisfy the desire of every living thing.*

God is simply generous beyond words. He is superfluous and superabundant in His supply. He does not just give us life. He gives us life *more abundantly* (John 10:10). He does not just bless. He blesses us till we do not have room enough to contain it (Malachi 3:10). His desire is to lavishly pour out gifts on His people, giving them good measure, pressed down, shaken together, and running over (Luke 6:38)!

Make no mistake about it: *God wants all His people to prosper exceedingly, and in today's terms, become millionaires.* God is not just concerned with your eternal well-being. He also wants you to have a life of wealth and prosperity here on earth right now.

ABRAHAM, LAZARUS, AND THE RICH MAN

In the sixteenth chapter of Luke's gospel, Jesus tells a real story involving three real people who once walked the face of the earth. They are Abraham, Lazarus, and the rich man. Typically, it is an account used to illustrate the reality of heaven and hell. But this story tells us about much more than eternity. It also gives insight into how we should live on the earth, because each one of the characters represents three types of people in the world today.

The rich man represents the group that I call the *ungodly rich*. They are those people who, though they are very rich in worldly goods, they are poor where God is concerned. They love money, but not God. They go after money, but they do not go after God. This set of people abounds in the world today.

They seek money at the expense of their soul and pay no attention to the God who made them. They foolishly forget that they came into the world naked and they will one day leave without any of their earthly possessions. The rich man enjoyed the best that the world had to offer, but he lost out on eternity. In this, he was so unwise. Compared to eternity, all the years we spend on earth are like a tiny drop in the ocean. He was foolish to jeopardize his eternal wellbeing for the pleasures of this temporary world.

Lazarus represents the group that I call the *godly poor*. Lazarus was a righteous man, but he did not enjoy the blessings of God's material provision while on earth. He represents those Christians who believe that riches are only to be expected in the sweet by and by. As far as they are concerned, it doesn't matter if they face defeat and poverty on earth as long as heaven awaits them. Lazarus gained heaven, but he lost out on what he could have enjoyed in the earth.

Lazarus' philosophy sounds nice and noble, but the truth is, it is not God's perfect will for His people. It is merely the traditions of men that have been passed on from one generation of religious folk to the other. But it is definitely not scriptural!

God's perfect will for His people can be seen in the life of Abraham, the great father of faith with whom the Lord God made a covenant (Genesis 17:1-2). Abraham represents the godly rich.

Abraham gained heaven, and he enjoyed the best of earth. He did not lose out on anything that God had to offer in this world or the next. He was rich and righteous. He loved God with all of his heart, and as a result, he was greatly blessed with material possessions. God prospered him mightily. On the earth, he was rich in silver and gold, and at death, heaven awaited him. Though Lazarus was better off than the rich man, he did not experience God's best. Abraham's life reflects the abundant and eternal life that God offers us in Christ Jesus.

YOU BELONG TO ABRAHAM'S CAMP!

Like Abraham, wealth and riches are your covenant privileges, and heaven is your home when you leave this earth. Jesus secured for you a life of abundance on earth, as well as a glorious eternity with Him in heaven. Do not settle for anything less than God's best!

As far as God is concerned, if you are in a covenant relationship with God through faith in Christ Jesus, *you should be wealthy,* and in *Seven Secrets of Bible-Made Millionaires,* I will show you just how you can!

Using the lives of some of Scripture's most famous millionaires as vivid illustrations, I will reveal seven powerful secrets of the Bible-made millionaires of old—people such as Millionaire Abraham, Millionaire Isaac, Millionaire David, and Millionaire Solomon, to name a few. Their million-dollar, God-inspired secrets are practical, time-proven principles for success that you will be able to apply to your life right away. You will discover exactly how you, too, as they did, can claim the wealthy portion that God has stored up for His righteous ones.

I decree in the name of our Lord Jesus Christ: The days of living from hand to mouth, paycheck to paycheck, are over. You are about to cross over from the wilderness of *just enough* or *a little more than enough* to the promised land of *much more than enough*. You are about to move from the *below* level to the *above only* level; from *lower or middle class* to the *topmost of the upper class*. You are about to enter into the realm of super-abundance where your cup of financial blessings continually runs over ... non-stop!

Chapter 1

Why God Wants You Wealthy

Now I want to make it very clear from the beginning that *Seven Secrets of Bible-Made Millionaires* is not just another *how-to-get-rich book*. This is why I have intentionally qualified the word *millionaire* with the phrase *Bible-made*. While God wants you to be wealthy, *it matters to Him how and why you get your wealth.*

How you get your wealth has eternal consequences. The ungodly rich who become wealthy by their human power alone do so at the expense of their soul. Though they gain fame and wealth in this life, they will lose out in the world to come. You saw this in the example of the rich man in Jesus' story.

There are many millionaires in the world today who neither know nor reverence God. So if you want to make millions or billions outside of God, it is very possible. But this book is not just about making millions. *It is about making millions through God's power and for God's purpose.*

There are two types of millionaires in the world today: (1) self- or manmade millionaires, and (2) Bible-made millionaires. Financially, both are the same. All millionaires possess material assets totaling at least one million dollars or more. But this is where their similarities end.

Man-made millionaires are those who get their wealth through *man's power* (i.e., human ability) alone. They hardly acknowledge or give God credit for the acquisition of their riches. Instead, they largely attribute their fame and wealth to their human connections, intellect, skill, and strength.

If you ask them, they'll tell you that the power of their own hand got them wealth. They do whatever they like with "their" money. They totally leave God out of the equation. Some of them are atheists and do not even believe in the existence of God. An interviewer once asked a famous billionaire about what he thought of God, to which he arrogantly answered, "I do not have any evidence about that!"

On the other hand, a Bible-made millionaire is a person to whom God has *given the power to get wealth*. This is because he has a covenant relationship with God through faith in Christ Jesus. The wealth of a Bible-made millionaire is first and foremost a product of God's *enabling* rather than human *engineering*.

The Bible-made millionaire knows beyond a shadow of doubt that he got his success and wealth by the power of God's hand. He knows that his best efforts could not have gotten him anywhere in life. He could have or achieve nothing if God did not give it to him. "*A man can receive nothing unless it has been given to him from heaven*" (John 3:27).

Millionaire Joseph stands out as one of the most prominent Bible-made millionaires. Sold into slavery at a tender age by his jealous brothers, Joseph ultimately became the second most powerful man in all of Egypt. Yet, not once did he claim to be a self-made man. Revealing his identity to his shocked and shamefaced brothers, Millionaire Joseph is careful to attribute both his fame and wealth exclusively to God.

> And God sent me before you to preserve a posterity for you in the earth, and to save your lives by a great deliverance. So now it was not you who sent me here, but God; and ***He has made me a father to Pharaoh, and lord of all his house, and a ruler throughout all the land of Egypt.***
>
> Genesis 45:7-8, emphasis mine

As far as he was concerned, his wealth and influential political status was God's making, not his own. This way of thinking is fundamental to becoming a Bible-made millionaire. Understand from the very beginning that you owe your wealth and success to God and God alone.

In this regard, a Bible-made millionaire realizes that his riches are not directly his own. Instead, he understands that he is just a steward of God's money. He knows he has a responsibility to use God's money in whatever way that He instructs him. Millionaire Joseph realized that God had made him rich and famous primarily to preserve His chosen people in the earth. His wealth was not for his own selfish ends. This is the huge difference between self-made millionaires and Bible-made millionaires.

A self-made millionaire will live for himself. But a Bible-made millionaire will live for the One who made Him, and he will put his wealth to God's use. So, in this book, I will not teach you how to get rich just for the sake of being rich. I will teach you how to become a millionaire God's way and for God's reasons.

God is a God of purpose. There is a reason for everything He does. God does not just want you to be wealthy for the sake of having money. There are certain God-ordained reasons why He wants to prosper you financially. *Every dollar that God gives you has a divine assignment attached to it.* You cannot spend the money that He gives you just any way you want. You must spend your God-given wealth according to His will.

Unless you fully understand the reason for your wealth, you are most likely to abuse it. So before I reveal the secrets of the Bible-made millionaire, I want to first make you understand why God wants you to be wealthy.

1. YOUR WEALTH IS FOR KINGDOM EXPANSION.

> "Again proclaim, saying, 'Thus says the LORD of hosts: "**My cities shall again spread out through prosperity**; The LORD will again comfort Zion, And will again choose Jerusalem."'
>
> Zechariah 1:17, emphasis mine

One of the foremost reasons why God prospers His people is for the expansion, or *spreading out,* of His kingdom. Earlier I mentioned that money was crucial to the fulfillment of our Lord's ministry in the earth. He had people (partners) who ministered to Him financially and whose monetary contributions helped Him accomplish His earthly work.

> Now it came to pass, afterward, that He went through every city and village, preaching and bringing the glad tidings of the kingdom of God. And the twelve were with Him, and certain women who had been healed of evil spirits and infirmities—Mary called Magdalene, out of whom had come seven demons, and **Joanna the wife of Chuza, Herod's steward, and Susanna, and many others who provided for Him from their substance.**
>
> Luke 8:1-3, emphasis mine

Thousands of years later, things have not changed. Money is still needed to carry on the work of the Lord in the earth. The more prosperous God's people are, the more empowered we will be to take the gospel to the ends of the earth. The gospel of God's kingdom will be preached throughout the whole earth with unprecedented speed.

Through the prosperity, the affluence, and the wealth of believers, the good news of salvation in Christ will *spread* to the unsaved in every nation on earth. All men will have the opportunity to receive His wonderful gift of salvation.

The most important thing to God is the souls of men. All the wealth of the world put together cannot be compared to the value of a human soul. Humans were so important to God that He paid the ultimate price to redeem us. God wants you to give souls a top priority in your heart because souls are His top priority!

Typically, you invest money in the things that are most important to you. No matter your financial status now, you should give actively to kingdom-advancing projects. Your money is primarily for the funding of the propagation of the gospel—it is your covenant duty to give generously to fund the preaching of the gospel. The whole world must hear the gospel before Christ's return, and it will take money to do it. The more financially empowered Christians are, the more accelerated the work will be.

2. YOUR WEALTH IS TO HELP OTHERS.

> Command those who are rich in this present age not to be haughty, nor to trust in uncertain riches but in the living God, who gives us richly all things to enjoy. Let them do good, that they be rich in good works, ready to give, willing to share.
>
> 1 Timothy 6:17-18

Your wealth is for *sharing*. It is not for *hoarding*. The purpose of godly prosperity is not to amass wealth for self-gain, but to apply wealth to meet human need.

God made this point clear right from the beginning as He was preparing His people to possess the land flowing with milk and honey. One of the first things He told them was that when they became wealthy, they should remember the poor and care for those in need.

> "... Except when there may be no poor among you; for the LORD will greatly bless you in the land which the LORD your God is giving you to possess as an inheritance—only if you carefully obey the voice of the LORD your God, to ob-

> serve with care all these commandments which I command you today. For the LORD your God will bless you just as He promised you; you shall lend to many nations, but you shall not borrow; you shall reign over many nations, but they shall not reign over you. If there is among you a poor man of your brethren, within any of the gates in your land which the LORD your God is giving you, you shall not harden your heart nor shut your hand from your poor brother, but you shall open your hand wide to him and willingly lend him sufficient for his need, whatever he needs."
>
> Deuteronomy 15:4-9

God's purpose to eradicate poverty among His people will be accomplished as *those who have* share with *those who have not*. Through this process of generous exchange, ultimately no one will lack anything that they need. Then will the prophetic word, "*... when there may be no poor among you; for the LORD will greatly bless you...*" will be powerfully fulfilled among believers everywhere.

This was a principle that the early church mastered. As a result, they lacked nothing. Every member was adequately supplied, and they had plenty left over for outreach to the world around them.

> Now all who believed were together, and had all things in common, and sold their possessions and goods, and divided them among all, as anyone had need.
>
> Acts 2:44-45

> Now the multitude of those who believed were of one heart and one soul; neither did anyone say that any of the things he possessed was his own, but they had all things in common. And with great power the apostles gave witness to the resurrection of the Lord Jesus. And great grace was upon them all. Nor was there anyone among them who lacked; for all who were possessors of lands or houses sold them, and brought the proceeds of the things that were sold, and laid them at the apostles' feet; and they distributed to each as anyone had need.
>
> Acts 4:32-35

It is no wonder that the early Christians were extremely successful and made a great impact through their ministry. Your wealth is not to elevate yourself above others or put yourself in a class all by yourself. It is to reach out to those in need that they may partake of the goodness of God upon your life.

3. YOUR WEALTH IS FOR YOUR CHILDREN'S INHERITANCE.

> A good man leaves an inheritance to his children's children.
>
> Proverbs 13:22a

God gives you wealth so that your children may be well taken care of. He provides for your children through you. As far as God is concerned, a person who neglects to care for his family is worse than an infidel.

> But if any provide not for his own, and specially for those of his own house, he hath denied the faith, and is worse than an infidel.
>
> 1 Timothy 5:8, KJV

In contrast, a good man is one who not only provides for his household, but also leaves an inheritance for his children and his grandchildren long after he is gone. It is an abomination for the seed of the righteous to beg for bread because God has empowered the righteous to get wealth and store up riches for their children.

Millionaire Abraham was a good man who left a great inheritance for his son Isaac. God blessed him in all things to the extent that he was very rich in cattle, in silver, and in gold (Genesis 13:2; 24:1). But Abraham's wealth did not end with him. He passed all of it on to his son. Genesis 25:5 says, *And Abraham gave all that he had to Isaac.* Abraham gave all his great wealth—his cattle, silver, and gold—to his son Isaac. Consequently, Isaac, being enriched by the wealthy inheritance that his father bequeathed to him, was mightily blessed of the Lord and prospered exceedingly.

Your wealth is not just for your consumption. It is for your children's inheritance. When you are about to leave this world at a good old age, plan to leave an inheritance that will make your children bless you from their hearts even generations after.

Do not plan to depend on social security in your old age. Do not see yourself becoming a liability to your children, either. Rather, see yourself blessing them mightily—giving houses, properties, businesses to them. Millionaire Abraham did it. You can do it, too!

Purpose in your heart that your children, by reason of the inheritance you leave them, will have a good head start in life. They will not struggle the way you did. They will not go through the pain that you went through. Pave the way for their bright future by leaving them a fat inheritance. This is another reason why God wants you wealthy.

4. Your Wealth Is for the Abundant Supply of All Your Needs.

> But money answers everything.
>
> Ecclesiastes 10:19b

God is a responsible Father. He has made daily provision for all your needs. You are the dependent of a dependable God who does not want you to be in want of anything. So He gives you money to answer or cater to every material need that you might have.

Needs vary from one person to the other, but whatever your need is, God is more than able to accommodate it. As a child of the Most High God, you are not permitted to lack anything in this life because God is capable of supplying **all** your needs according to His riches in glory (Philippians 4:19).

Remember those who walked closely with Jesus? They lacked **no thing**. One day, Jesus asked them, *"When I sent you without money bag, knapsack, and sandals, did you lack anything?" So they said, "Nothing"* (Luke 22:35).

They lacked nothing. *Everything* that they needed was abundantly supplied to them. God wants your testimony to be like theirs. He wants you to be able to look at your life and confidently declare, "**I lack nothing!**"

But though He has gone to great lengths to provide for His people, many believers still languish in want and lack. He gave His people the power to get wealth; He filled the earth with His riches so that they could live in abundance and plenty (Psalm 104:24); He gave them all things richly to enjoy (1 Timothy 6:17), yet many beloved saints are not enjoying God's rich provision. What an irony. What a waste!

It is an abomination for the children of a rich and righteous God to beg for bread. God cares for you and is committed to supplying all your needs. God is an abounding God, and it grieves Him to see you suffer needless lack. But He is glad and pleased when you prosper: *Let them shout for joy and be glad, who favor my righteous cause; and let them say continually, "Let the LORD be magnified, who has pleasure in the prosperity of His servant"* (Psalm 35:27). He loves it when you take full advantage of His great provision, which He has made available for you.

5. YOUR WEALTH IS FOR YOUR DEFENSE.

> For wisdom is a defense as money is a defense,
> But the excellence of knowledge is that wisdom
> gives life to those who have it.
>
> Ecclesiastes 7:12

The word *defense* means "shadow," "shade," or "protection." Poverty or lack can make a person vulnerable to all kinds of evil. Money, on the other hand, shields you from the ravages of this world that make life uncomfortable, unbearable, and unproductive. It protects or defends against malnutrition, underdevelopment, and so forth. It will protect you from the evils that ravage a person as a result of poverty.

> The rich man's wealth is his strong city; The destruction of the poor is their poverty.
>
> Proverbs 10:15

Wealth here is likened to a strong fortified city. On the other hand, destruction comes upon the poor because he lacks such fortification. Lack of money makes a person open, vulnerable, and subject to innumerable ills. For instance, lack of money to buy food will make a person vulnerable to malnutrition and ultimately disease. There is an unmistaken connection between a person's lifespan and his financial status. God wants you to have a good and full life. That is why He has made wealth available to you.

Recently the queen of England celebrated her eightieth birthday; her good health has a lot to do with her financial security. Her contemporaries in impoverished conditions could hardly live that long or that well. He gives you wealth so that even in old age, you will not be defenseless against harsh conditions. You will be well-armed with all the resources that you need to live well, flourish, and keep bearing fruit … still being a blessing to the world. Money allows you to attain your full potential. It is a tool in God's hands to give you a long and full life.

We live in a volatile and unstable world, but through wealth, God will shield you from destruction and preserve your life. Remember, Millionaire Joseph, through wealth, was empowered to preserve the lives of many people in the midst of a terrible famine.

Money will also defend you against human tyranny. God gives you money so that you can be in a position of strength and power. A person in lack is extremely vulnerable and at the mercy of those more affluent than he. But no one can discriminate against a wealthy man. He cannot be oppressed or pushed over.

6. YOUR WEALTH IS FOR DEBT-FREE LIVING.

> The rich rules over the poor, And the borrower is servant to the lender.
>
> Proverbs 22:7

God does not want you to be indebted to anyone. According to Scripture, the only debt that we are to owe is love (Romans 13:8). Debt brings bondage, and Jesus came to set us free from sin and every kind of bondage, including indebtedness.

Whichever way you look at it, the debtor serves, or is in bondage to, the lender. Your position as a covenant child of God is that of a lender. You are not a borrower. Deuteronomy 28:12 says, *The LORD will open to you His good treasure, the heavens, to give the rain to your land in its season, and to bless all the work of your hand. You shall lend to many na-*

tions, but you shall not borrow. Do you now understand that those who do not have a covenant with God should borrow from you, not the other way around?

Many believers are in debt today. They are at the mercy of their unbelieving lenders. Some believers, like Lazarus, love God deeply, yet they live as beggars in the earth, looking up to the ungodly rich for sustenance. This is an abomination. It is not your portion in life. You are meant to lend to the heathen, not the other way around!

But by the decree of God, I declare things are about to change. If you are in debt, through the principles that I will share in this book, the Lord God will break every yoke of debt from off your neck, and you will assume your rightful position as lender in Jesus' mighty name.

God has empowered you so greatly that you will not just lend to men, you will lend to nations, just as God's Word declares. Yes, I really believe we will get to that point in the Body of Christ where wealthy believers will singlehandedly lend to the nations or peoples of the world. God's Word cannot be broken. If He said it, it will happen!

SOME OF THE BIBLE'S MOST FAMOUS BIBLE-MADE MILLIONAIRES

The fact that God wants His people to be wealthy is evident by the extraordinary way that He prospered His people in Bible times. The Bible is full of accounts of people whom God made so very rich. Note that the Bible states clearly that they became wealthy by God's enabling, not by human engineering. This is what makes them "Bible-made millionaires." Their vast wealth and assets are documented so that it is obvious why in today's terms they would be considered millionaires by every standard. The profile of some of the Bible's most wealthy includes:

❖ MILLIONAIRE ABRAHAM

God prospered Millionaire Abraham to the point that he became extremely rich in cattle, in silver, and in gold (Genesis 13:2).

Genesis 24:1 sums it up when it says: *The LORD had blessed Abraham in all things.* I love how *The Living Bible* puts it: *God blessed him in every way.* Note that the Bible clearly states that it was God who blessed Abraham. This clearly indicates that his wealth was the product of God's enabling, not his own engineering.

❖ MILLIONAIRE ISAAC

Millionaire Isaac greatly benefited from the prosperity of his father, Abraham. However, Isaac was not rich just because he was born with a silver spoon in his mouth. The Bible clearly records that his prosperity was a direct result of God's blessing. Genesis 25:11 says, *And it came to pass, after the death of Abraham, that God blessed his son Isaac. And Isaac dwelt at Beer Lahai Roi.*

So great was God's hand of blessing on Millionaire Isaac that he was able to prosper exceedingly in the most adverse of circumstances. During a time of great famine, the Bible says, *Isaac sowed in that land, and reaped in the same year a hundredfold; and the LORD blessed him. The man began to prosper, and continued prospering until he became very prosperous; for he had possessions of flocks and possessions of herds and a great number of servants. So the Philistines envied him"* (Genesis 26:12-14).

❖ Millionaire Jacob

Like his father and grandfather before him, Millionaire Jacob was also a man greatly prospered by the Lord. Of him the Bible says, *Thus the man became exceedingly prosperous, and had large flocks, female and male servants, and camels and donkeys* (Genesis 30:43).

Millionaire Jacob, or Israel, as he was later known, continued to prosper even in old age living in Goshen: *So Israel dwelt in the land of Egypt, in the country of Goshen; and they had possessions there and grew and multiplied exceedingly* (Genesis 47:27).

❖ Millionaire Joseph

Concerning Millionaire Joseph, the Bible says that he had gained great glory in Egypt (Genesis 45:13). By the enabling and blessing of God, this former slave boy and prisoner, became Egypt's second most powerful man, and by all implications, also one of her wealthiest.

> Then Pharaoh said to Joseph, "Inasmuch as God has shown you all this, there is no one as discerning and wise as you. You shall be over my house, and all my people shall be ruled according to your word; only in regard to the throne will I be greater than you." And Pharaoh said to Joseph, "See, I have set you over all the land of Egypt." Then Pharaoh took his signet ring off his hand and put it on Joseph's hand; and he clothed him in garments of fine linen and put a gold chain around his neck. And he had him ride in the second chariot which he had; and they cried out before him, "Bow the knee!" So he set him over all the land of Egypt. Pharaoh also said

> to Joseph, "I am Pharaoh, and without your consent no man may lift his hand or foot in all the land of Egypt."
>
> Genesis 41:39-44

❖ MILLIONAIRE JOB

Millionaire Job was a righteous man who loved and reverenced the Lord dearly. He was reputed to be the richest man living in his region during his time: *His possessions were seven thousand sheep, three thousand camels, five hundred yoke of oxen, five hundred female donkeys, and a very large household, so that this man was the greatest of all the people of the East* (Job 1:3).

Although at one time in his life, Job faced terrible satanic attack, God's hand of blessing ultimately came through for him. Not only did God restore Job to his original position of wealth, He restored back to this Bible-made millionaire so much more than he ever had before!

> Now the LORD blessed the latter days of Job more than his beginning; for he had fourteen thousand sheep, six thousand camels, one thousand yoke of oxen, and one thousand female donkeys.
>
> Job 42:12

❖ MILLIONAIRE DANIEL

God blessed this captive eunuch in a strange land until he became one of the most powerful and prosperous men in the land. Millionaire Daniel prospered mightily during the regime of four Babylonian kings.

First, he prospered during the tenure of Nebuchadnezzar, who *...promoted Daniel and gave him many great gifts; and he made him ruler over the whole province of Babylon, and chief administrator over all the wise men of Babylon* (Daniel 2:48).

Second, in King Belshazzar's reign, the king *...gave the command, and they clothed Daniel with purple and put a chain of gold around his neck, and made a proclamation concerning him that he should be the third ruler in the kingdom* (Daniel 5:29).

Finally, the Bible says that Millionaire Daniel prospered greatly during the regime of King Darius and King Cyrus: *So this Daniel prospered in the reign of Darius and in the reign of Cyrus the Persian* (Daniel 6:28).

❖ MILLIONAIRE BOAZ

Millionaire Boaz was a very wealthy landowner and husbandman who was also a direct descendant of King David: *There was a relative of Naomi's husband, a man of great wealth, of the family of Elimelech. His name was Boaz* (Ruth 2:1).

❖ MILLIONAIRE DAVID

From his humble beginnings as a shepherd boy, God raised up Millionaire David to become Israel's greatest king and one of her wealthiest men. Second Samuel 12:8 plainly states that everything he had was given to him by God.

King David was extremely wealthy, to the point that he singlehandedly contributed, from his own personal money, $85 million worth of gold and $20 million worth of silver to the construction of the temple of the Lord.

> "And now, because of my devotion to the Temple of God, I am giving all of my own private treasures to aid in the construction. This is in addition to the building material I have already collected. These personal contributions consist of millions of dollars of gold from Ophir and huge amounts of silver to be used for overlaying the walls of the buildings. It will also be used for the articles made of gold and silver and for the artistic decorations. Now then, who will follow my example? **Who will give himself and all that he has to the Lord?"**
>
> 1 Chronicles 29:3-5, TLB, emphasis mine

Because of the blessing of God, Millionaire David lived a long and prosperous life. *He died in a good old age, full of days and riches and honor...* (1 Chronicles 29:28).

❖ MILLIONAIRE SOLOMON

Of all the Bible-made millionaires recorded in Scripture, Millionaire Solomon stands out as the most famous. He was by far Israel's wealthiest king. The Bible says that he *...surpassed all the kings of the earth in riches and wisdom* (1 Kings 10:23; see also 2 Chronicles 9:22).

So enormous was Solomon's wealth that during his reign, it was said that silver and gold were as readily available as the stones on the ground!

> Also the king made silver and gold as common in Jerusalem as stones, and he made cedars as abundant as the sycamores which are in the lowland.
>
> 2 Chronicles 1:15

Just think about it. Money was so plentiful that it was as easy to have as picking up stones from the ground! In 1 Kings 10:14-27 (TLB), Millionaire Solomon's enormous wealth is listed in greater detail.

> Each year Solomon received gold worth a quarter of a billion dollars, besides sales taxes and profits from trade with the kings of Arabia and the other surrounding territories. Solomon had some of the gold beaten into two hundred pieces of armor (gold worth $6,000 went into each piece) and three hundred shields ($1,800 worth of gold in each). And he kept them in his palace in the Hall of the Forest of Lebanon.
>
> He also made a huge ivory throne and overlaid it with pure gold. It had six steps and a rounded back, with arm rests; and a lion standing on each side. And there were two lions on each step—twelve in all. There was no other throne in all the world so splendid as that one.
>
> All of King Solomon's cups were of solid gold, and in the Hall of the Forest of Lebanon his entire dining service was made of solid gold. (Silver wasn't used because it wasn't considered to be of much value!)
>
> King's Solomon's merchant fleet was in partnership with King Hiram's, and once every three years a great load of gold, silver, ivory, apes, and peacocks arrived at the Israeli ports.
>
> So King Solomon was richer and wiser than all the kings of the earth. Great men from many lands came to interview him and listen to his God-given wisdom. They brought him annual tribute of silver and gold dishes, beautiful cloth, myrrh, spices, horses, and mules.

> Solomon built up a great stable of horses with a vast number of chariots and calvary—1,400 chariots in all and 12,000 cavalrymen, who lived in the chariot cities and with the king at Jerusalem. Silver was as common as stones in Jerusalem in those days, and cedar was of no greater value than the common sycamore!

It is important for you to keep in mind that the Bible credits Solomon's incredible wealth 100-percent to God's enabling. First Chronicles 29:25 says, *So the LORD exalted Solomon exceedingly in the sight of all Israel, and bestowed on him such royal majesty as had not been on any king before him in Israel.*

It was God who exalted Solomon. It was He who bestowed upon him royal majesty that exceeded any of his predecessors, including his father, the great King David. Without God's power, Solomon could not have been as wealthy as he was. Solomon was by every means a Bible-made millionaire.

❖ MILLIONAIRE JEHOSHAPHAT

Millionaire Jehoshaphat was another king who became powerful and wealthy by the power of God's hand.

> Now the LORD was with Jehoshaphat, because he walked in the former ways of his father David; he did not seek the Baals, but sought the God of his father, and walked in His commandments and not according to the acts of Israel. Therefore the LORD established the kingdom in his hand; and all Judah gave presents to Jehoshaphat, and he had riches and honor in abundance.
>
> 2 Chronicles 17:3-5

He enjoyed a continual supply of presents and silver from tributaries, a great number of livestock, as well as valuable real estate.

> Also some of the Philistines brought Jehoshaphat presents and silver as tribute; and the Arabians brought him flocks, seven thousand seven hundred rams and seven thousand seven hundred male goats. So Jehoshaphat became increasingly powerful, and he built fortresses and storage cities in Judah. He had much property in the cities of Judah; and the men of war, mighty men of valor, were in Jerusalem.
>
> 2 Chronicles 17:11-13

As with the other Bible-made millionaires, King Jehoshaphat had riches and honor in abundance by reason of God's enabling. He prospered because God was with him.

❖ MILLIONAIRE HEZEKIAH

> Hezekiah had very great riches and honor. And he made himself treasuries for silver, for gold, for precious stones, for spices, for shields, and for all kinds of desirable items; storehouses for the harvest of grain, wine, and oil; and stalls for all kinds of livestock, and folds for flocks. Moreover he provided cities for himself, and possessions of flocks and herds in abundance; for **God had given him very much property.**
>
> 2 Chronicles 32:27-29, emphasis mine

Hezekiah was wealthy *because God had given him very much property.* Again it is clear from these verses that Millionaire Hezekiah had the wealth that he had because God gave it to him.

It's Time for *Millionaire You!*

If God prospered His people in ancient times, you can be sure that He wants to prosper you today. God does not change. Malachi 3:6 says, *"For I am the LORD, I do not change; therefore you are not consumed, O sons of Jacob."* His principles for wealth and success are never outdated. They are as good for us today as they were in Bible days. If you follow the same principles that the ancient Bible millionaires lived by, you will enjoy the success that they enjoyed.

When you diligently *imitate those who through faith and patience inherit the promises,* you will also get to your own promised land (Hebrews 6:12). God will give you the same results that He gave them … even more so because now you are God's heir in Christ Jesus. The Lord Jesus has gained for you wealth that is simply beyond human imagination.

> For you know the grace of our Lord Jesus Christ, that though He was rich, yet for your sakes He became poor, that you through His poverty might become rich.
>
> 2 Corinthians 8:9

Yes, dear friend, in Christ, you can become wealthier than any Old Testament saint ever was. So pay no attention to the devil when he bombards you with thoughts of fear, doubt, or insecurity, saying, "You cannot prosper. You are simply not smart enough. You are not in the right social class…."

Resist him strong in faith, saying, "Get behind me, satan. I can and will become the wealthy person that God has ordained me to be. God has done it before, and He is more than able and willing to do it again. He is the same yesterday, today, and forever!" (Hebrews 13:8).

Chapter 2

You've Got the Power!

> "And you shall remember the LORD your God, for it is He who gives you power to get wealth, that He may establish His covenant which He swore to your fathers, as it is this day."
>
> Deuteronomy 8:18

One of the first things you must understand and settle in your mind is that godly prosperity is not a matter of luck or chance. It is a matter of covenant.

There are some believers who do not doubt the fact that God wants them to prosper, but only to a certain degree. In their own "realistic" opinion, they feel that the millionaire status is only for some; it is not for all. They wonder, "Well, we can't all be leaders and millionaires. Even God said that the poor will not cease from the land. Is it really possible for every single Christian to become wealthy?"

If that has been your way of thinking, change it now! Know beyond any shadow of doubt that God wants **all** His people to be wealthy. Yes, super rich! He actually looks forward to a time when, as a result of His blessings, not one of His precious people would be poor, ... *when there may be no poor among you; for the LORD will greatly bless you in the land which the LORD your God is giving you to possess as an inheritance* (Deuteronomy 15:4).

As far as God is concerned, prosperity is not a random gift that He bestows on a select few. God made the blessings of Abraham available to *all those who are of faith*. No believer is more privileged than the other. No believer is excluded, because the power to get wealth is a matter of *covenant*; it is not a matter of *chance*.

> Just as Abraham "believed God, and it was accounted to him for righteousness." Therefore know that **only those who are of faith are sons of Abraham**.... So then **those who are of faith are blessed with believing Abraham**.... Christ has redeemed us from the curse of the law, having become a curse for us (for it is written, "Cursed is everyone who hangs on a tree"), that the blessing of Abraham might come upon the Gentiles in Christ Jesus, that we might receive the promise of the Spirit through faith.
>
> Galatians 3:6-14, emphasis mine

Those who are of faith are blessed with believing Abraham because as sons of Abraham they are entitled to the enormous wealth and blessings that he enjoyed from God. Are you in covenant with God through faith in Christ? Are you of faith? Then you are qualified for great riches!

Abraham was an extremely prosperous man. He is one of the first recorded Bible millionaires whose riches and assets were evidently documented in Scripture. Remember, as Genesis 13:2 clearly states, *He was very rich in livestock, in silver, and in gold.* Also, speaking of him to the family of his son's proposed bride, Abraham's oldest servant said:

> The LORD has blessed my master greatly, and he has become great; and He has given him flocks and herds, silver and gold, male and female servants, and camels and donkeys.
>
> Genesis 24:35

And according to Galatians 3, *those who are of faith are blessed with believing Abraham.* This means that every single believer … everyone who has received the Lord Jesus as their Lord and Savior … has access to the full blessings of Abraham. Regardless of your skill, skin color, social background, or the society in which you live, if you are of faith, Abraham's blessings are yours!

God told Abraham, *"I will make you a great nation; I will bless you and make your name great; and you shall be a blessing. I will bless those who bless you, and I will curse him who curses you; and in you all the families of the earth shall be blessed"* (Genesis 12:2-3).

If you are a believer in Christ Jesus, that word *"you"* stands for you! God will make *you* a great nation. God will bless *you* and make your name great; and *you* shall be a blessing. God will bless those who bless *you,* and He will curse him who curses *you*; and in *you* all the families of the earth shall be blessed!

There is no reason why Christians, who are in covenant relationship with God, should struggle and suffer financially. If God blessed Abraham and others under the Old Covenant in such an extraordinary way, how much more will He bless those of us who are in relationship with Him under the New Covenant, which has even better promises?

Do not say, "If only I had a better education, I *could* be rich;" "if only I had a different skin color;" "if only I came from an affluent family;" "if only ..." Forget all the *"if onlys"*! Nothing can work against you because God's power is working for you. *He has given you the power to get wealth.*

Regardless of who you are or where you live, you have what it takes to become a financial giant in the earth. God has taken away all the limits. You can be wealthy because God has given you the power to get wealth!

Friend, God is no respecter of persons. What He did for Abraham, He has done for you. He has *already* given you the power and the ability to get wealth. Get rid of the scarcity, or just-enough, mentality. Know for a fact that you can be wealthy. By covenant, you are destined to live an above-average lifestyle. You are ordained to live both richly and righteously in the earth.

God has given you *the power, or ability, to get wealth.*

Certainly, as far as God is concerned, every believer, without exception, can and should be prosperous. However, it is one thing for you to have access to wealth. It is another thing for you to take advantage of that access. This is why Deuteronomy 8:18 does not just say, God gave you wealth. It says God gave you *the power to get wealth*. If you want to really enjoy the riches that God has made available to you, you must be willing to lay hold of that power and put it to work.

The Bible-made millionaires of old enjoyed great wealth because they all harnessed their God-given power to get wealth and had great results to show for it. They did not sit down idly waiting for God to drop millions upon millions of dollar bills into their lap. Rather, they learned how to make maximum use of their God-given power and attain great success and wealth in life.

God has given you the power to get wealth so that you can get rid of poverty and mediocrity. Think about it. Would He give you the power to get wealth if He wanted you to be poor or live an average life? Absolutely not! Note that He did not say, "I give you the power to earn a living and have just enough to take care of your family." He said, "*I give you the power to get wealth … to be abundantly supplied; to be so very rich.*" Beloved, you do not belong to the lower or middle class. You belong to the "above only" class. You are destined to be on top, never beneath! (Deuteronomy 28:13).

If He made wealth available for all His people, it must displease God that only some are prospering financially. Only relatively few in the Body of Christ have been able to press into the abundance that God has stored up for the righteous. Countless others are struggling terribly in their finances. This is not how God meant for it to be.

Many are not enjoying the wealth that God made available because of sheer ignorance. They simply lack a revelation that they have been empowered by covenant to become wealthy. You need a revelation of the truth in God's

Word that He has stored up wealth for you. He has given every Christian the power to become prosperous and victorious in life. When you discover a working knowledge of the truth, you will prosper and flourish financially as you should.

PUTTING YOUR POWER TO WORK

Everything in heaven and on earth is strictly regulated by divine rules. God has principles that govern every sphere of life on earth. There are divine laws for health, wealth, success, victory, and so forth. Nothing happens by chance or haphazardly. Nothing works until you work it!

No matter how much you love God; no matter how much you fast and pray, go to church, or even serve God in one capacity or the other; if you disregard His principles in any area of life, you cannot enjoy His full plan for you in that area. If you want to become the Bible-made millionaire that God has ordained you to be, you must be prepared to operate God's principles for wealth to the fullest. Prepare to put your power to get wealth to work!

Many Christians are not enjoying the riches that are available to them because they are ignorant of or disregard God's laws regarding wealth. God upholds and rules the world by the word of His power. Anyone who does not do things according to His set laws cannot get the desired results out of life.

It is one thing to accept the Person of Christ. It is another thing to live by His principles. If you believe in the principles of the Lord Jesus but not in the Person of Jesus, you will make it big time in this world, but you will go to hell when you die. On the other hand, if you believe in the

Person of Jesus but do not accept and live according to His principles, you will be poor here on earth, though you will have eternal life with Jesus after you leave this world.

God's perfect plan is that you enjoy a life of abundance here on earth *and* spend eternity with Him in heaven. Jesus came to give us both eternal and abundant life. Eternal life comes when you accept the Lord Jesus as your Lord and personal Savior, and abundant life comes when you follow the principles of our Lord. So accepting His Person will secure you a place in heaven. But living by His principles will secure you abundant life upon the earth.

The laws of God that govern the earth will work for anyone who puts them to work. It may surprise you to know that many of the world's millionaires and motivational speakers actually live by principles of wealth gleaned from Scripture. Though they may not be His followers, they will enjoy His wealth because they follow Jesus' principles of prosperity. God's principles will work for anyone who observes them, just as the law of gravity works for all men, believers and non-believers alike.

I have read many books about millionaires and billionaires of the world. I have noticed that their secrets to success are actually taken from the pages of Scripture, although they hardly give God the credit. Many motivational speakers propound extraordinary prosperity and success, bringing theories that originate from God's Word.

One of the wealthiest motivational speakers in the United States today is Anthony Robbins, who came from a very poor background but is worth billions today. One of his favorite adages is, "If I can change your belief system, I can change everything." This profound statement actually reflects a fundamental principle in the Bible found in Proverbs 23:7, which says, *For as he thinks in his heart, so is he.*

Ironically, nonbelievers, those who do not know God, prosper by merely adopting His principles for success. Yet believers who know God but do not practice His wealth principles, though they have access to God's untold riches, struggle and suffer financially. I believe this is what the Lord meant when He said, "*...the sons of this world are more shrewd in their generation than the sons of light*" (Luke 16:8b).

If the unsaved can become millionaires and billionaires simply by practicing God's principles, how much more should believers who have access both to the principles of God and the Person of God?

It is a serious abomination for an unbeliever to outshine a child of the covenant. You are strategically positioned by covenant to prosper and be wealthy in life. The advantages that you have over unbelievers are so great. You have the mind of Christ; you have been blessed with spiritual blessings in heavenly places. He has given you the power to get wealth, and therefore you *should* prosper. It is an abomination for you not to. It is an error.

> There is an evil I have seen under the sun, As an error proceeding from the ruler: Folly is set in great dignity, While the rich sit in a lowly place. I have seen servants on horses, While princes walk on the ground like servants.
>
> Ecclesiastes 10:5-7

You are a child of the covenant. Wealth is your portion. God has laid before you an entire table of blessings. Unbelievers only have access to the crumbs that fall from your Father's table. Those who have access to only crumbs should not prosper more than you who are entitled to the feast itself! As a believer, you are set for a blessed life. If you do not prosper, it is your fault, not God's.

With the kind of provision that God has made, there is no reason why any child of God should live in lack. Understand that believers should be the ones on the Forbes' list of the world's richest. They should be the ones in the forefront of economic advancements, they should be the heads, and they should be the lenders … because they have access to the full table. Unbelievers do not!

Please get this: Wealth is yours by inheritance. If unbelievers can get wealthy merely from the crumbs that fall from your Father's table, how much more should you who have access to the sumptuous feast that is on the table itself?

The problem is that while those in the world are using the principles of God to get the best out of the *crumbs*, the believers are sitting idly by, waiting for manna to fall out of heaven! Well, I have news for you—manna has stopped falling from heaven! We have crossed the Jordan and now live in the Canaan land era where wealth abounds, waiting for you to harvest it by the power that God has given you.

After the Israelites crossed the Jordan River into their land of promise, the Bible tells us that manna stopped falling from heaven (Joshua 5:12). From that point on, it was their responsibility to work the land and tap its invaluable resources.

No matter how full a cow's breasts are, if the rancher isn't prepared to milk the cow, he cannot get one drop of milk from her. So also, the milk and honey of the Promised Land is only guaranteed to flow to those who are prepared to *milk* it. To enjoy the great wealth that God has stored up for you, you must take hold of God's principles for wealth and apply them to your life.

Disregard of God's principles of wealth has cost many Christians their financial destiny. Only those who obey God's commands will command riches and wealth in the earth. The seven secrets that I will discuss in this book are some of the key principles ordained by God that govern wealth. As you operate them, you will prosper beyond your wildest dreams!

Part 2

The Seven Secrets of Bible-Made Millionaires

I will give you the treasures of darkness And hidden riches of secret places, That you may know that I, the LORD, Who call you by your name, Am the God of Israel.

Isaiah 45:3

Chapter 3

Secret #1: Make God Your First Priority

> "But seek first the kingdom of God and His righteousness, and all these things shall be added to you."
>
> Matthew 6:33

Nowhere in the Scriptures are you told to go after money. Instead, God's Word commands you to seek God *first,* then money, and every good thing of life will inevitably follow.

Bible-made millionaires realize that the process of becoming wealthy begins by being rich toward God. A strong relationship with God is the foundation for blessed and prosperous living. Bible-made millionaires devote their heart first and foremost to God. As a result, God causes His wealth to abound to them.

The Bible's most prominent millionaires had one thing in common: They loved and sought God above anything else.

Millionaire Abraham's love walk with God was the force behind his great wealth. Genesis 17:1-2 says, *When Abram was ninety-nine years old, the LORD appeared to Abram and said to him, "I am Almighty God; walk before Me and be blameless. And I will make My covenant between Me and you, and will multiply you exceedingly."* Note that God did not say, "Go after money, and I will make you rich." He said, "*Walk before Me and be blameless.*" In other words, "Make your relationship with Me your top priority, and I will do the rest. I will multiply and increase you in all things."

Millionaire David was affectionately called by God Himself, *a man after mine own heart* (Acts 13:22 KJV). Remember that King David was extremely wealthy, so much so from his own personal money that he singlehandedly contributed $85 million worth of gold and $20 million worth of silver to the construction of the temple of the Lord.

King David was a man who truly loved God more than his possessions. He proved it by giving himself and all he had to the Lord. Though Millionaire David started out as a shepherd boy, as he walked with God in love, God established His covenant with him and promoted him above his peers. He gave him an eternal throne.

Millionaire Solomon, King David's son and Israel's wealthiest king, also began his journey to fame by devoting his heart to the Lord. First Kings 3:3-14 says:

> **And Solomon loved the LORD, walking in the statutes of his father David**, except that he sacrificed and burned incense at the high places. Now the king went to Gibeon to sacrifice there, for that was the great high place: Solomon of-

> fered a thousand burnt offerings on that altar. At Gibeon the LORD appeared to Solomon in a dream by night; and God said, "Ask! What shall I give you?" …
> Then God said to him: "… Behold, I have done according to your words; see, I have given you a wise and understanding heart, so that there has not been anyone like you before you, nor shall any like you arise after you. And I have also given you what you have not asked: both riches and honor, so that there shall not be anyone like you among the kings all your days. So if you walk in My ways, to keep My statutes and My commandments, as your father David walked, then I will lengthen your days" (emphasis mine).

Also, concerning Millionaire Uzziah, David's direct descendant and one of Judah's wealthiest kings, it was said, *He sought God in the days of Zechariah, who had understanding in the visions of God; and as long as he sought the LORD, God made him prosper* (2 Chronicles 26:5). This powerful man was, among other things, a great inventor, an innovator, and a mighty general. And the degree to which he prospered depended largely upon the degree to which he sought God.

Some Christians forcefully seek to *lay up* treasures for themselves in the earth, yet they are so *laid back* when it comes to their relationship with God. They foolishly think within themselves, "Let me make money first, then later I will have more time for God." They are more committed to their business or career than they are to God. They give a 100-percent commitment to their personal pursuits, but give God very little of themselves.

Such people would never dare to miss a board meeting or arrive late at their secular jobs. Yet they are pathetically slack when it comes to the things of God. They come to church when it is convenient for them. They hardly have any time for personal devotion. Their priorities in life are misplaced. They struggle, toil, and expend undue energy trying to make money. They want to acquire riches at all costs—at the expense of other people, their marriage, their family, and even at the expense of their relationship with God. Such people never eat the fruit of their labor. They may record progress in the beginning, but their end is never good. Beware that you do not fall into this trap.

Mary Kay Ash, a fine Christian woman and founder of Mary Kay Cosmetics, was by every standard a Bible-made millionaire. Her life philosophy and formula for success was to *put God first, family second, and career third.* Using this formula, before her passing on November 22, 2001, Mary Kay built a Fortune 500 multi-billion-dollar enterprise. She was by far one of America's most influential business women of recent times. Mary Kay Cosmetics continues to thrive today, with over 600,000 independent beauty consultants worldwide!

Friend, Mary Kay's outstanding success proves that it pays to put God first even in today's hectic society. This is the only way up. Please do not overdo it when it comes to money. Do not, in the name of seeking success, neglect your walk with God. The Word of God is clear: Do not labor to be rich. Do not make money your life's pursuit.

> Do not overwork to be rich; Because of your own understanding, cease! Will you set your eyes on that which is not? For riches certainly make themselves wings; They fly away like an eagle toward heaven.
>
> Proverbs 23:4-5

The truth is: You do not have to struggle or join the rat race before you stand out in life. All you need to do is maintain intimacy with God. When your love walk with God is intact, you will not need to sweat to get wealth. Your love for God secures His blessing upon your life. Riches will flow to you naturally, with ease.

> The blessing of the Lord—it makes [truly] rich, and He adds no sorrow with it [neither does toiling increase it]
>
> Proverbs 10:22, AMP

If you want to become a Bible-made millionaire, you must give your heart to God in full devotion. Nothing should be done with greater zeal than what you do for God. Jesus said, "*For where your treasure is, there your heart will be also*" (Luke 12:34). In other words, you will treasure what you devote your heart to the most. And when you give your heart to God in love and total devotion, He will make the treasures of His hand abound to you.

Money May Give You Luxuries, But Only God Can Give You Life!

Bible-made millionaires make God their top priority because they realize one indisputable fact of life: Money can give a person the world's finest *luxuries*. But money cannot give anyone *life!* Only God can.

This is why Jesus warned in Luke 12:15:

> "Guard yourselves and keep free from all covetousness (the immoderate desire for wealth, the greedy longing to have more); for a man's life does not consist in and is not derived from possessing overflowing abundance or that which is over and above his needs" (AMP).

Your life isn't sustained by *money*. It is sustained by your *Maker!* You exist by God's power; therefore it is to Him, not money, that you owe your full devotion. *Your commitment to your work, endeavors, or enterprises must never be greater than your commitment to God.* So give God the best and most of your time and energies.

I once heard of a rich man whose wife was gravely ill. He would gladly give anything he had to save her. He took her to the best doctors in the world, sparing no expense. But eventually he was hit with the sad reality that though his wealth could get her the best medical treatment, his money could not buy her life. Ultimately she died. In indescribable grief and utter desperation, he cried, "*Shame on you, money, shame on you. You are vain and worthless!*"

Indeed, money has its limits. It can give you comfort and pleasure, but it cannot give you life. Realize this, and devote your life totally to the One by whose power you live, move, and have your very being (Acts 17:28).

If you seek wealth and neglect your relationship with God, remember that your time in this world is only for a while. One day you will leave this earth and stand face to face with your Maker. Riches cannot buy you a mansion in heaven. You can only secure a place with God in eternity when you give your heart to Jesus in full surrender. He is the only One who can prepare a mansion in heaven for you. To all who trust Him as their Lord and Savior, He says, "*In My Father's house are many mansions; if it were not so, I would have told you. I go to prepare a place for you*" (John 14:2). Those who spent all their life pursuing wealth and ignoring God will lose out big time!

> "For what profit is it to a man if he gains the whole world, and loses his own soul? Or what will a man give in exchange for his soul?"
>
> Matthew 16:26

> "For what profit is it to a man if he gains the whole world, and is himself destroyed or lost?"
>
> Luke 9:25

If you want to become a Bible-made millionaire, God must be your number-one priority. Do not let temporary material things distract you from the reality of the eternal world. When you passionately go after God, He will reveal to you where the hidden treasures are. With ease and no stress, you will locate the wealth that God has stored up for you in the earth.

BIBLE-MADE MILLIONAIRES ARE GOD-DIGGERS, NOT GOLD-DIGGERS.

Bible-made millionaires esteem God above anything or anyone else, and as a result, they give Him their wholehearted devotion. This is what it really means to make God your top priority: You value, or treasure, Him above all else. When you treasure God, you will *dig* for God; you will go after the things of God. But if you treasure gold, you will dig for gold; you will go after material things. *Bible-made millionaires are God-diggers, not gold-diggers.*

If you pursue business or monetary interest above spiritual things, it is proof that you are a gold-digger, not a God-digger, and this is idolatry before God. Jesus clearly said that you cannot serve God and money. God alone must be your sole focus. Everything else should be secondary.

Do not let your relationship with God suffer because of your desire to prosper. Go for God, and you will have gold in abundance. Go for gold and neglect God, and eventually the riches you think you have will leave you.

HOW DO YOU MAKE GOD YOUR NUMBER-ONE PRIORITY?

Matthew 6:33 answers this question as plainly as possible: "But seek first the **kingdom of God** and **His righteousness**" (emphasis mine).

You make God your number-one priority by making God's kingdom and His righteousness your sole focus in life. More than anything else, aim at and strive after (1) His kingdom, or His way of doing things, and (2) His righteousness, or His way of being, i.e., His nature.

Simply put, make God your number-one priority by making it your life's pursuit to be like God both in your character and conduct. It is God's desire that you resemble Him in all things, to be perfect as He is perfect and holy as He is holy. "*Therefore you shall be perfect, just as your Father in heaven is perfect*" (Matthew 5:48).

1. SEEK HIS KINGDOM—DO THINGS GOD'S WAY!

Bible-made millionaires *do not seek things. They seek God's way of doing things.* Please understand that there are only two ways of handling every matter of life: God's way or man's way, *the way of the Word* or *the way of the world.* There are no in-betweens.

Those who make God their priority have committed themselves to exclusively doing things God's way. If God is your number-one priority, you will not run your business or pursue your career after the pattern of the world. Instead, you will conduct all your life affairs, including your endeavors, in the ways of God.

You will not step on other people's toes to climb up the corporate ladder, you will not falsify documents to secure business contracts, and you will strictly allow yourself to be guided and governed by the righteous principles of God's Word. Your commitment to doing things in God's upright way will ultimately cause His wealth to abound in your house.

> Praise the LORD! Blessed is the man who fears the LORD, Who delights greatly in His commandments. His descendants will be mighty on earth; The generation of the upright will be blessed. Wealth and riches will be in his house, And his righteousness endures forever.
>
> Psalm 112:1-3

Bible-made millionaires are straight in their dealings. They are not crooked. They fully embrace God's way and forsake the way of the world. They demonstrate their love and reverence to God by absolute obedience to His Word. Bible-made millionaires understand that money is merely a tool in their hand to carry out God's commands. So they give importance to the commands of God and not the demands of money. In other words, they disregard the counsel or way of thinking of the ungodly, they do not join the multitudes to commit sin, and they do not move with critical and negative people.

> Blessed is the man Who walks not in the counsel of the ungodly, Nor stands in the path of sinners, Nor sits in the seat of the scornful; But his delight is in the law of the LORD, And in His law he meditates day and night. He shall be like a tree Planted by the rivers of water, That brings forth its fruit in its season, Whose leaf also shall not wither; And whatever he does shall prosper.
>
> Psalm 1:1-3

It is amazing what some people, even believers, will do for money. Some will compromise the holy standards of God's Word just to get rich. For instance, I have noticed how some Christians emigrating from other countries into the United States greatly compromise God's Word regarding marriage. It is pathetically common for some to marry U.S. citizens on a contractual basis in order to regularize their stay. They feel that unless they are citizens of the U.S., they cannot prosper in this land, so they choose to do whatever it takes to get legal status. They compromise and engage in all kinds of illegal activities to make headway.

Beloved, this is not the way of the Bible-made millionaire. A Bible-made millionaire will never compromise God's Word for anything. He will only act in line with the Word. Get this straight: You are not to do anything for money. Instead, *whatever you do, do all to the glory of God* (1 Corinthians 10:31).

You do not have to break God's Word in order to prosper. Respect His Word, and He will honor you. You do not need to be an American citizen to make it big in America. The God who prospered and elevated the Bible-made millionaires of old in foreign lands will do the same for you. Only honor God's Word in all things. Do not sell your birthright for anything!

As a young man, Millionaire Daniel was taken as a captive to Babylon, where he served King Nebuchadnezzar. Even at the threat of death, he refused to compromise his commitment to God's Word. On one such occasion, when Daniel and his friends first arrived at the king's palace, they were offered food and drink from the king's private kitchen. These included foods that God's Word clearly forbade them from eating. In reverence to God's command, both Daniel and his friends refused to eat the food; instead they asked for vegetables and water.

> But Daniel purposed in his heart that he would not defile himself with the portion of the king's delicacies, nor with the wine which he drank; therefore he requested of the chief of the eunuchs that he might not defile himself.
>
> Daniel 1:8

God honored Daniel by granting him supernatural knowledge, understanding, and the power to interpret dreams and visions (Daniel 1:17). This knowledge and wisdom came in handy for Daniel when King Nebuchadnezzar gave him the seemingly impossible task of interpreting the king's dream with no details about the dream. Daniel's execution date was set in the event that he failed at the task. Daniel did not fret. No! He remembered that when you stand for God's Word, in the day of adversity God will stand for you, too! In a night vision, God revealed all of King Nebuchadnezzar's dreams to Daniel together with the interpretations. This not only saved Daniel's life, but it also caused the king to prostrate himself before Daniel, a foreign hostage, a Jewish boy in Babylon!

> Then King Nebuchadnezzar fell on his face, prostrate before Daniel, and commanded that they should present an offering and incense to him. The king answered Daniel, and said, "Truly your God is the God of gods, the Lord of kings, and a revealer of secrets, since you could reveal this secret." Then the king promoted Daniel and gave him many great gifts; and he made him ruler over the whole province of Babylon, and chief administrator over all the wise men of Babylon.
>
> Daniel 2:46-48

As a result of the spirit of excellence that God gave Daniel, he became a governor over one hundred and twenty-seven provinces in Babylon. God honored him greatly because he honored God's Word. Because he loved his God and would not compromise His Word, Millionaire Daniel, a foreigner in the land of Babylon, was promoted to great prominence and wealth. Ultimately God elevated him even above the natural-born citizens of the land.

I know of a precious brother who came to the U.S. with a visitor's visa and immediately got involved in the real-estate market. This brother made over $500,000 in a short period of time. When he went to the bank to deposit his earnings, he was informed that he would have to be reported to the U.S. Department of Immigration. His response to the bank manager was, "Please, go ahead. I look forward to speaking with the immigration officials about my stay in the U.S." Some time later when the brother reported to the immigration office, the officer looked at the success this brother had attained in the U.S. and offered him a green card (permanent residency).

Beloved, Acts 10:34 says, *God shows no partiality.* He is no respecter of persons. It does not matter whether or not you are a citizen of the land in which you live. Your color doesn't matter; neither does the color of your documents! It's your belief system that matters. Even in America, he who fears Him and walks righteously is accepted and can succeed. If you want the divine force of blessing to deliver the riches of the earth for you, you must walk before God in uprightness and truth.

2. Seek His Righteousness—Be Like God.

As wonderful as it is, having millions of dollars is not the greatest thing in life. The greatest thing in life is to know God and understand His ways.

> Thus says the LORD: "Let not the wise man glory in his wisdom, Let not the mighty man glory in his might, Nor let the rich man glory in his riches; But let him who glories glory in this, That he understands and knows Me, That I am the LORD, exercising lovingkindness, judgment, and righteousness in the earth. For in these I delight," says the LORD.
>
> Jeremiah 9:23-24

The more you know God, the more like Him you will become. And the more you become like God, the more of His glory, power, and wealth will find expression in your life. Bible-made millionaires recognize this, and therefore, *they make knowing God, not acquiring money, their top priority in life.*

In your journey to wealth, from the onset make up your mind that nothing will be as important to you as your relationship with God. Determine never to allow your personal devotion with God to suffer because of crowded business schedules. Make your time with Him top priority. Time is one of life's greatest assets. When you give God your time, you prove that He has first place in your life. Give your time and energies to diligently seeking God in prayer, worship, and the study of His Word.

Many people come to God because of what they want to get from Him. But Bible-made millionaires come to God because of what they want to give Him—their heart! When you give God your heart, you prove that nothing is more valuable to you than God.

God meant more to Millionaire David than anything. The Book of Psalms reveals that he was a man who intently pursued intimacy with the Lord.

> Evening and morning and at noon I will pray, and cry aloud, And He shall hear my voice.
>
> Psalm 55:17

> O God, You are my God; Early will I seek You; My soul thirsts for You; My flesh longs for You In a dry and thirsty land Where there is no water.
>
> Psalm 63:1

Deep love for God caused David to compose love songs for Him and sing them joyfully, regardless of the circumstances that surrounded him.

> I will bless the LORD at all times; His praise shall continually be in my mouth. My soul shall make its boast in the LORD; The humble shall hear of it and be glad. Oh, magnify the LORD with me, And let us exalt His name together.
>
> Psalm 34:1-3

These words came from the depths of a heart full of love.

As one of the highest ranking officials in the land, Millionaire Daniel must have been a very busy man. Yet this did not stop him from faithfully spending time with God in prayer three times a day. So great and true was his love for God that Daniel maintained this daily routine of seeking God even at the risk of his own life.

> So these governors and satraps thronged before the king, and said thus to him: "King Darius, live forever! All the governors of the kingdom, the administrators and satraps, the counselors and advisors, have consulted together to establish a royal statute and to make a firm decree, that whoever petitions any god or man for thirty days, except you, O king, shall be cast into the den of lions. Now, O king, establish the decree and sign the writing, so that it cannot be changed, according to the law of the Medes and Persians, which does not alter." Therefore King Darius signed the written decree. Now when Daniel knew that the writing was signed, he went home. And in his upper room, with his windows open toward Jerusalem, he knelt down on his knees three times that day, and prayed and gave thanks before his God, as was his custom since early days.
>
> Daniel 6:7-11

Daniel loved God more than life itself. He would not let anything or anyone interfere with his relationship with God. As a result, not only did God deliver him from death, He also promoted him and made him very great.

> Then Daniel said to the king, "O king, live forever! My God sent His angel and shut the lions' mouths, so that they have not hurt me, because I was found innocent before Him; and also, O king, I have done no wrong before you." Now the king was exceedingly glad for him, and commanded that they should take Daniel up out of the den. So Daniel was taken up out of the den, and no injury whatever was found on him, because he believed in his God. So this Daniel prospered in the reign of Darius and in the reign of Cyrus the Persian.
>
> Daniel 6:21-23, 28

Friend, please understand this principle clearly: *You can't obtain or sustain godly prosperity without a genuine devotion to the Lord.* Begin now to have solitary times with God fixed into your daily schedule. Deliberately cultivate a love relationship with God.

Think about it. You make and keep appointments to see your doctor, employer, and clients because you know that you have much to gain from them. How much more would you stand to gain when you fix and keep appointments with your Father and your God?

As the song says, *no one can do you like Jesus*! No one can impact your life as He can. He is your glory and the One who lifts your head (Psalm 3:3). Promotion and lifting in life comes from Him alone (Psalm 75:6). In His hand alone lies the power to lift up and to cast down!

There is no doubt about it. It is in your best interest to make your walk with God your priority. No business meeting should be important enough to keep you from God's presence. When you daily invest in your relationship with God, you will excel in your secular endeavors. I have said it time and time again, it is impossible for you to give your all to God and fall short in your secular job. The love that Abraham, David, and Daniel had for God made them men of dominion, and God blessed them beyond millions!

Do not let anything come in between you and God. Do not ever forget Him. Do not stop seeking Him.

> "And you shall remember the LORD your God, for it is He who gives you power to get wealth, that He may establish His covenant which He swore to your fathers, as it is this day. Then it shall be, if you by any means forget the LORD your God, and follow other gods, and serve them and worship them, I testify against you this day that you shall surely perish."
>
> Deuteronomy 8:18-19

As a new arrival to the United States, the Lord strongly cautioned me not to get caught up in the hustle and bustle of American life. I must keep my relationship with Him top priority. Nothing and no one should be allowed to chip away at the time that I spend with Him. He spoke to me so clearly one day, saying, *"Don't camp around men; camp around Me, and you will never be a beggar."* Since then, God has taken me from one level of prosperity to another. There is no human that can claim credit for the blessings that I am enjoying. I am totally a God-made man!

Friend, do not pursue money. Pursue God! Do not labor to be rich. *Instead, labor in the Word of God.* Grow more intimately with Him through daily, consistent Bible study and prayer. If you seek wealth, it will flee from you. But if you seek God, money will locate you and stay with you. *A faithful man will abound with blessings, but he who hastens to be rich will not go unpunished* (Proverbs 28:20).

Bible-made millionaires understand that except the Lord build their businesses, their companies, and their careers, no matter who they know or what they do, they will not succeed!

> Unless the LORD builds the house, They labor in vain who build it; Unless the LORD guards the city, The watchman stays awake in vain.
>
> Psalm 127:1

Therefore, do not pursue a career, build a business, or forge a partnership at the expense of your relationship with God. Put God first! No venture or enterprise on earth, no matter how promising or lucrative, should take God's place in your heart. Commit yourself to the Lord today, saying, *"God, You are number one in my life. Give me the grace to seek You above all else, all the days of my life, in Jesus' name, amen!"*

Chapter 4

Secret #2: Be a Visionary: Know Your God-Given Purpose and Stick to It

> ...who has saved us and called us with a holy calling, not according to our works, but according to His own purpose and grace which was given to us in Christ Jesus before time began...
>
> 2 Timothy 1:9

No doubt making God your sole focus is the fundamental secret of becoming a Bible-made millionaire. But loving God alone cannot bring you into the prosperity that God has in store for you.

The fact that you love God doesn't mean prosperity is automatically on its way. As we discovered in the case of Lazarus, there are many people who genuinely love God, yet they are wallowing in poverty. It is not that they are unfaithful to God. It is just that they have not taken the subsequent steps required to tap into the wealth that He has stored up for them.

One quality that is most predictive of financial success is what I call *clarity* and *intensity of purpose*. Bible-made millionaires are very clear and determined about their life's purpose. They are not unsure of what they want to be or do.

The great King David did not just prosper because he was a man after God's heart. He was a candidate for God's blessings because he was a man of purpose. He devoted his life to accomplishing God's cause. He was a man who fought the battles of the Lord. Speaking of Millionaire David, Abigail (who later became David's wife) said:

> "**For the LORD will certainly make for my lord an enduring house, because my lord fights the battles of the LORD**, and evil is not found in you throughout your days. Yet a man has risen to pursue you and seek your life, but the life of my lord shall be bound in the bundle of the living with the LORD your God; and the lives of your enemies He shall sling out, as from the pocket of a sling. And it shall come to pass, when the LORD has done for my lord according to all the good that He has spoken concerning you, and has appointed you ruler over Israel."
>
> 1 Samuel 25:28b-30, emphasis mine

David secured an enduring house from the Lord who blessed him greatly because he embraced his God-ordained purpose. He did not fight his own battles; he did not follow his own agenda. He fought only the battles of the Lord. He carried out God's plans.

Millionaire Joseph excelled in power and wealth as Egypt's second most powerful man because he understood that God had ordained him to save many people from hunger and death. He understood that he was in Egypt on a divine assignment. He had no personal agenda of his own. God's will was his command. Speaking to his brothers, he said:

> "And God sent me before you to preserve a posterity for you in the earth, and to save your lives by a great deliverance. So now it was not you who sent me here, but God; and He has made me a father to Pharaoh, and lord of all his house, and a ruler throughout all the land of Egypt."
>
> Genesis 45:7-8

One of life's greatest tragedies is a life without purpose. It is dangerous to be alive and not know why you are alive, why you were created, and what you are supposed to be doing with your life on a daily basis. Martin Luther King Jr. said, "If a man has no reason or purpose for living, he is not fit to live." Another wise man said that "a man without a purpose is like a ship without a rudder—a waif, a nothing, a no man." Friend, if you want to amount to something in life, if you want to be great, if you want to become the millionaire that God intends you to be, you must understand your God-ordained purpose.

What Is Purpose?

Purpose is the original intent and reason for the creation or existence of a thing. Scripturally, your purpose is the plan of God for you—what He created you to accomplish in the earth. It is a personal and individual life projection of God's plan for you.

When a manufacturer embarks upon a new invention, what is his first step? He first conceives a vision, which is the purpose for the invention. He first answers the question, "What is this thing going to do for people, and what is it going to accomplish for the world?" That is the purpose of the thing.

Until a manufacturer knows the purpose of the object, he has no design, and he has no invention. And so it is with your awesome God. He is your Creator, and He is the One who determined your purpose even before you were born. The Lord says in Jeremiah 1:5:

> "Before I formed you in the womb I knew you; Before you were born I sanctified you; I ordained you a prophet to the nations."

The prophet Jeremiah did not choose or construct his purpose. His purpose was already ordained by God even before his parents ever met.

The Lord Jesus, whom we follow and adore, lived a life of purpose. He said in John 18:37, *"For this cause I was born, and for this cause I have come into the world, that I should bear witness to the truth."* Jesus understood the reason why He was born, and so should you. You ought to know the cause for which you were born.

Your God-given purpose is the key to a life of prosperity. Without purpose, life will lack value and will be burdensome. Without purpose, life has no meaning, no significance, and no hope. It is petty and pointless. Where purpose is not known, opportunities to prosper will be abused. They will not be taken advantage of. Precious time, energy, and resources will also be wasted. But when you know your life's purpose, you will maximize and make the most of every opportunity and resource at your disposal.

It is your duty to ask God to reveal to you His vision and plan for your life. Only then can your life be meaningful and productive. Nothing matters more than knowing God's purpose for your life. The Word of God gives example after example of saints who prospered and enjoyed great success because they lived according to God's will and purpose for their lives.

As a young boy, God revealed His great plan for Millionaire Joseph through two prophetic dreams.

> Now Joseph had a dream, and he told it to his brothers; and they hated him even more. So he said to them, "Please hear this dream which I have dreamed: There we were, binding sheaves in the field. Then behold, my sheaf arose and also stood upright; and indeed your sheaves stood all around and bowed down to my sheaf." And his brothers said to him, "Shall you indeed reign over us? Or shall you indeed have dominion over us?" So they hated him even more for his dreams and for his words. Then he dreamed still another dream and told it to his brothers, and said, "Look, I have dreamed another dream. And this time, the sun, the moon, and the eleven stars bowed down to me." So he told it to his father and his brothers; and his father rebuked him and said to him, "What is this dream that you have dreamed? Shall your mother and I and your brothers indeed come to bow down to the earth before you?" And his brothers envied him, but his father kept the matter in mind.
>
> Genesis 37:5-11

God revealed to him that he would reign and be placed in a position of great dominion. During the most trying times of his life, when he served as a slave in Potiphar's house and was unjustly imprisoned, his dreams gave him strength to live from day to day. He knew that regardless of what he faced today, his tomorrow was glorious. God had shown him that he would be a distinguished leader, and nothing could stop His purpose from being fulfilled. Because he did not lose sight of his purpose, Millionaire Joseph lived to fulfill his dream. God lifted him out of the prison and placed him in the palace. He became the second most powerful man in all of Egypt. Without a doubt, Joseph's dreams were a strong factor in his prosperity. His God-given vision helped to propel him to a position of extraordinary wealth, success, and power.

Millionaire Abraham's journey to fame was also backed by a God-given vision.

> After these things the word of the LORD came to Abram in a vision, saying, "Do not be afraid, Abram. I am your shield, your exceedingly great reward."
> But Abram said, "Lord GOD, what will You give me, seeing I go childless, and the heir of my house is Eliezer of Damascus?" Then Abram said, "Look, You have given me no offspring; indeed one born in my house is my heir!" And behold, the word of the LORD came to him, saying, "This one shall not be your heir, but one who will come from your own body shall be your heir." Then He brought him outside and said, "Look now toward heaven, and count the stars if you are able to

> number them." And He said to him, "So shall your descendants be." And he believed in the LORD, and He accounted it to him for righteousness.
>
> Genesis 15:1-6

It was Millionaire Isaac's God-given vision that sustained him and propelled him to great prosperity during a time of great famine. Though he had every reason to give up, he kept going on because God had appeared to him saying, "*Do not go down to Egypt; live in the land of which I shall tell you. Dwell in this land, and I will be with you and bless you; for to you and your descendants I give all these lands, and I will perform the oath which I swore to Abraham your father. And I will make your descendants multiply as the stars of heaven; I will give to your descendants all these lands; and in your seed all the nations of the earth shall be blessed*" (Genesis 26:1-4).

Isaac was totally unaffected by the pain and economic hardship of the land. While others were *going under*, Isaac kept *going over!* While others were *winding down*, he was *warming up!* While they were *suffering*, he was *soaring!* *He sowed in that land, and reaped in the same year a hundredfold; and the LORD blessed him. The man began to prosper, and continued prospering until he became very prosperous; for he had possessions of flocks and possessions of herds and a great number of servants. So the Philistines envied him* (verses 12-14).

How about Millionaire Jacob? His encounter at Bethel was by all means the defining moment of his life.

> Now Jacob went out from Beersheba and went toward Haran. So he came to a certain place and stayed there all night, because the sun had set. And he took one of the stones of that place and put it at his head, and he lay down in that place to sleep. Then he dreamed, and behold, a ladder was set up on the earth, and its top reached to heaven; and there the angels of God were ascending and descending on it. And behold, the LORD stood above it and said: "I am the LORD God of Abraham your father and the God of Isaac; the land on which you lie I will give to you and your descendants. Also your descendants shall be as the dust of the earth; you shall spread abroad to the west and the east, to the north and the south; and in you and in your seed all the families of the earth shall be blessed. Behold, I am with you and will keep you wherever you go, and will bring you back to this land; for I will not leave you until I have done what I have spoken to you."
>
> Genesis 28:10-15

Before he had his vision, Jacob was homeless and penniless. All he had was a wooden staff (Genesis 32:10). But a few years later, God had blessed him greatly and he *became exceedingly prosperous, and had large flocks, female and male servants, and camels and donkeys* (Genesis 30:43).

There are many modern-day Bible-made millionaires who, like the saints of old, attribute their success in life and ministry largely to their God-given purpose. These people know God's plan for their life and stick to it. They do not venture into a place that God did not show them.

One such person is my mentor, Dr. David Oyedepo, one of God's leading generals in Africa and the world today. On May 2, 1981, as he communed with God in prayer, the Lord showed him a stunning eighteen-hour long vision in which he saw a line of battered, tattered, beaten, and oppressed people who were all wailing in agony. So vivid and real was this sight that he soon found himself crying along with them.

He also felt compelled to ask the Lord why the people whom he saw were in such a pitiable and sorrowful state. He heard God say, "In the beginning it was not so." The Lord then gave him a clear mandate saying, *"The hour has come to liberate the world from all oppressions of the devil through the preaching of the word of faith, and I am sending you to undertake this task."*

This mandate was Dr. Oyedepo's divine purpose. It was the reason why God had created him. He was to be an instrument in God's hands to help bring mankind back to the position of dignity and honor that God intended for man from the beginning of creation. It is a mandate that he has been running with for the past twenty-five years.

That glorious 1981 encounter was no doubt the key turning point in his life and ministry. His life took a radically progressive turn. Since then, his dynamic, pace-setting ministry has experienced phenomenal success, which includes a large worldwide network of churches. Chief among these is *Faith Tabernacle*, the ministry's magnificent 50,000-seat sanctuary, situated in Lagos, Nigeria. God has also blessed him with a world-class university, publishing house, and world mission center. There is no question about it—his progress and prosperity in life is directly linked to his ability to embrace and execute his mandate to the fullest.

To become a Bible-made millionaire, you need a God-given vision, which births purpose. When there is no projection, there will be no progression in life. God can only take you to a place that you can see. If you cannot see it, you cannot reach it. Someone once said that without a purpose, "life is motion without meaning, activity without direction, and events without reason." Without God-given vision, people are grounded to the point of destruction.

> Where there is no vision, the people perish: but he that keepeth the law, happy is he.
>
> Proverbs 29:18 KJV

There are sad examples of people who lived outside of their divine purpose, and destruction was their portion. King Saul was such a person. God had chosen him to serve Him as king over His people, Israel. But only two years into his assignment, King Saul deviated from his God-given purpose, and against Prophet Samuel's strict orders, he presumptuously acted in the capacity of a priest and offered a burnt offering to the Lord. God had called him to be a king, not a priest. Crossing into a territory that God did not give him cost King Saul his destiny. He fell from royal status—he lost his majesty and his crown.

> So Saul said, "Bring a burnt offering and peace offerings here to me." And he offered the burnt offering. Now it happened, as soon as he had finished presenting the burnt offering, that Samuel came; and Saul went out to meet him, that he might greet him. And Samuel said, "What have you done?" And Saul said, "When I saw that the people were scattered from me, and that you did not come within the days appointed, and

> that the Philistines gathered together at Michmash, then I said, 'The Philistines will now come down on me at Gilgal, and I have not made supplication to the LORD.' Therefore I felt compelled, and offered a burnt offering." And Samuel said to Saul, "You have done foolishly. You have not kept the commandment of the LORD your God, which He commanded you. For now the LORD would have established your kingdom over Israel forever. But now your kingdom shall not continue. The LORD has sought for Himself a man after His own heart, and the LORD has commanded him to be commander over His people, because you have not kept what the LORD commanded you."
>
> 1 Samuel 13:9-14

There is also the account of King Uzziah. He, too, paid dearly for doing what God did not ordain him to do. Like Saul, he deviated from his kingly role and arrogantly acted as a priest.

> But when he was strong his heart was lifted up, to his destruction, for he transgressed against the LORD his God by entering the temple of the LORD to burn incense on the altar of incense. So Azariah the priest went in after him, and with him were eighty priests of the LORD—valiant men. And they withstood King Uzziah, and said to him, "It is not for you, Uzziah, to burn incense to the LORD, but for the priests, the sons of Aaron, who are consecrated to burn incense. Get out of the sanctuary, for you have trespassed! You shall have no honor from the LORD God."

> Then Uzziah became furious; and he had a censer in his hand to burn incense. And while he was angry with the priests, leprosy broke out on his forehead, before the priests in the house of the LORD, beside the incense altar.
>
> 2 Chronicles 26:16-19

Uzziah had begun well. He was a Bible-made millionaire who had at one time loved God and sought Him with all his heart. Yet, he ended badly because, in arrogance, he deviated from the path that God had charted for him.

Saul and Uzziah's fate will never be your portion in Jesus' mighty name! Stick to your God-ordained purpose. Your life does not belong to you. You belong to God. Love Him and live for His purpose alone, and you will prosper all the days of your life.

ENORMOUS PROVISION ALWAYS FOLLOWS DIVINE VISION.

Do not forget that God gives you wealth for His purpose. Always remember that the money that He gives you is not yours. It is His. And it is to be put to His use. So to qualify for wealth, you must understand and walk in your God-ordained purpose. If you want to be a Bible-made millionaire, you must locate God's purpose for your life. When you know your purpose, the wealth of heaven will flow toward you.

When you discover your purpose and the special assignment God has for you, then you can excel. No matter how much you love God, if God ordained you to be a lawyer, you cannot prosper maximally as a doctor. God ordained me to be a pastor, and that is why I am prospering. There are so many who are running other people's races. And provision only follows vision. If you go to a place or pursue a profession that God did not assign you, there will be no provision … no wealth there.

How Can I Know God's Purpose for My Life?

God created you *on purpose*, not by accident. Like all the Bible-made millionaires of old, God has a plan for you. He wants to reveal to you His special plan for your life, which He had even before you were born.

Obviously since God is the One who made you, only He can reveal your purpose to you. So to know your purpose, you must seek God. Let us examine just how you can do this.

1. Seek to Know Your Purpose in Prayer.

In Jeremiah 29:11, God says, "I know the plans I have for you." God has a plan for you. All you need to do is inquire of Him in prayer and ask Him to show you His plan for your life. Your inquiry will lead to the discovery of your God-given purpose. Simply ask God, "Why did You create me? What is my purpose in the earth?"

For best results, you should make your inquiry in a quiet place. I personally suggest that you take some time off to seek God. Go to a solitary place where you know that you will not be disturbed. Remember Dr. David Oyedepo's story? His divine purpose was revealed to him during a time of solitary prayer. Separate yourself and call out to Him in prayer. Lay down your own prior plans and sincerely seek to know only God's heart and mind for you.

> "Call to Me, and I will answer you, and show you great and mighty things, which you do not know."
>
> Jeremiah 33:3

When you call out to God in sincerity of heart with no hidden agenda, when you honestly tell him that you want His will alone to be accomplished in your life, God will surely answer you! He will show you things about your life and future that you never knew before.

In 1987, as I worshipped and prayed before the Lord, He said to me, *"I have not called you to work in the secular world, but to be My mouthpiece. Millions of Americans are roaming the streets without a shepherd, and I am sending you to be their under shepherd while I remain the Chief Shepherd."* I further inquired of God, "You're calling me to be a pastor, but what do You want me to preach, because a jack of all trades is a master of none?"

Please understand that God is not a God of confusion; He is a God of specifics. He will not just give you a general idea of His plan. He will reveal it to you in great detail so that you cannot miss it. For instance, if you ask God about your purpose and He says He has appointed you to serve in the health-care industry, it is your responsibility to make further inquiries and ask, "Which area, God?" God knows it is a huge field, and He will be more than willing to reveal more details to you.

In my case, after I made further inquiry of the Lord, He then spoke to my heart that He was giving me the mandate to preach His message of dominion in Christ to lost and oppressed humanity. He said that through His ministry at my hand, many would experience the reality of being restored back to the original position of power and authority that man had in God before Adam's fall.

If you earnestly ask God to reveal to you the reason why you were created, He will answer you. When the Apostle Paul had an encounter with Jesus on his way to Damascus, the first question he asked was, *"Lord, what do You want me to do?"* (Acts 9:6). Then the Lord Jesus answered him immediately saying, *"Arise and go into the city, and you will be told what you must do."*

Jesus will answer you immediately when you make an inquiry of Him. The challenge that many believers have with hearing Him is their level of spiritual development. Believers who love God, who dwell in the Word of God, who are in constant fellowship with God, who obey Him, who have a quiet and meek spirit, who fear God, and who are not living in sin hear Him speedily.

However, those who are living in sin, who do not have a genuine love for God, and who are seeking God's blessings rather than God's purpose will have a harder time hearing God. Like Habakkuk, I pray that you will stand your watch, set yourself on the rampart, and wait to see what God will say to you regarding your purpose in life (see Habakkuk 2:1).

Beloved, do not delay further. You need to know why God put you on this earth. Do not live another day while running another person's race. Get in the presence of God, humbly bow down, and say to your Maker, "*Lord, what is Your plan for me? What would You have me do? Please reveal to me my God-given life purpose. Open my ears and heart to discern Your will for my life. Give me the grace, dear Lord, and the tools to live a life that is in line with the reason You created me. May You and You alone be glorified through my life. In Jesus' name I pray, amen."*

Then embrace whatever He reveals to you with all your heart. Start running with your God-given purpose. As you do, He will prosper you mightily because divine provision always accompanies vision. Your life will begin to take shape and have color like never before. You will be a megastar!

2. KNOW YOUR PURPOSE THROUGH YOUR GIFTS AND TALENTS.

> But to each one of us grace was given according to the measure of Christ's gift. Therefore He says: "When He ascended on high, He led captivity captive, and gave gifts to men."
>
> Ephesians 4:7-8

> For I wish that all men were even as I myself. But each one has his own gift from God, one in this manner and another in that.
>
> 1 Corinthians 7:7

God has endowed every one of His people with divine gifts, talents, and abilities. What you enjoy doing and are good at is the gift, talent, and skill that has been deposited in you. They are what you are wired for, what you naturally gravitate toward.

Your gifting gives a strong indication as to your life's purpose. God doesn't give you gifts just for the sake of it. No talent is useless. God endows you with your talents for a specific purpose—so that you may work or *do business* with them in a way that serves His purpose.

> Therefore He said: "A certain nobleman went into a far country to receive for himself a kingdom and to return. So he called ten of his servants, delivered to them ten minas, and said to them, 'Do business till I come.'"
>
> Luke 19:12-13

Ultimately your ability to faithfully use your gifts will bring you into the greatness and wealth that God has ordained for you. Proverbs 18:16 says, *A man's gift makes room for him, and brings him before great men.*

There are also spiritual gifts that point to God's call on your life. Some examples of such gifts are: preaching, teaching, hospitality, leadership, and so forth.

> Having then gifts differing according to the grace that is given to us, let us use them: if prophecy, let us prophesy in proportion to our faith; or ministry, let us use it in our ministering; he who teaches, in teaching; he who exhorts, in exhortation; he who gives, with liberality; he who leads, with diligence; he who shows mercy, with cheerfulness.
>
> Romans 12:6-8

Friend, when you discover your divine gifts and talents, consider them as your unique fingerprinting, your divine purpose from the Almighty. They are not in you by accident. They are tools that God has intentionally deposited in you to help you carry out His divine purpose for your life. When you use these gifts and talents for the specific purposes God intended, you will unlock your full potential and awaken to the greatness, wealth, and prosperity that is your inheritance in Christ.

However, don't expect that being talented alone will make you rich. There are many talented poor people. Your gift will make room for you … it will create opportunities, but it will not make you rich unless you take full advantage of those opportunities. Do not let them slip by. Do not sit idly with your gifts. *Stir up the gift of God which is in you* (2 Timothy 1:6). Embrace every opportunity to put your gifts to work; then you will prosper.

> A gift is as a precious stone in the eyes of him that hath it: whithersoever it turneth, it prospereth.
>
> Proverbs 17:8, KJV

Turn your gift … put it to use as often as opportunity presents itself, and it will prosper you. But if you sit still with it, it will do you no good. So your primary responsibility in life is to be faithful with everything that God has given you, including your gifts and talents. If you use your gifts and talents faithfully, if you do business with them as He has commanded, they will bring you great wealth.

Millionaire Joseph was gifted with the ability to interpret dreams. He was also a very wise and skilled administrator. But he did not sit still with his gifts. He embraced every opportunity that he had to interpret dreams. He also did his very best serving as an administrator first in Potiphar's household, and later on in the prison. Ultimately it was Joseph's faithful and diligent use of his gifts that brought him prosperity and promoted him to the position of administrator over all of Egypt, to be the second most powerful man in the land.

> And Pharaoh said to his servants, "Can we find such a one as this, a man in whom is the Spirit of God?" Then Pharaoh said to Joseph, "Inasmuch as God has shown you all this, there is no one as discerning and wise as you. You shall be over my house, and all my people shall be ruled according to your word; only in regard to the throne will I be greater than you." And Pharaoh said to Joseph, "See, I have set you over all the land of Egypt." Then Pharaoh took his signet ring off his hand and put it on Joseph's hand; and he clothed him in garments of fine linen and put a gold chain around his neck. And he had him ride in the second chariot which he had; and they cried out before him, "Bow the knee!" So he set him over all the land of Egypt.
>
> Genesis 41:38-43

Your gifts will surely make room for you! They will pave the way to unprecedented success and wealth. Discover them and put them to God's use, and you will prosper. But you must remember, your gifts, talents, and abilities are ideally suited only for the purpose for which God has created you. If you try to use them for anything else, you will fail miserably! What will bring godly wealth to you is when you find yourself operating in the center of your expertise (your divine purpose) while obeying God's principles. When you use your gifts and talents to accomplish His perfect purpose, God can't help but bless you. He is faithful and cannot deny Himself!

3. KNOW YOUR PURPOSE THROUGH YOUR DESIRE.

> Delight yourself also in the LORD, And He shall give you the desires of your heart.
>
> Psalm 37:4

The desires that God births in your heart are a strong indication of His purpose for your life. Very often, after you have sought the Lord in prayer about your life's purpose, God will respond by giving you deep heart desires. When you delight yourself in doing God's will, when you set yourself to fulfill His plan alone, God will birth good, wholesome aspirations in your heart.

What are you passionate about? What do you aspire to become? What problem confronting mankind would you like to see solved? If you have noticed that you have a particular passion or desire to accomplish something, it may be a good pointer to your life's purpose.

Growing up, I had always desired to become an ambassador. I desired to travel the nations of the world. At the time, I had no idea that this desire was God-birthed. However, when later in life God gave me my divine mandate of preaching His message of dominion to the world, I had no problem embracing it with excitement. Today I am living the fulfillment of those desires. I am an ambassador for Christ, traveling throughout the world as an emissary of His life-changing Word.

From her childhood, my wife always loved to read and write. She could read the King James Version of the Bible by the time she was in first grade. As a young girl growing up, she would rather read a book than play with dolls. Reading and writing were second nature to her, and she dreamed of becoming an author when she grew up. This desire was God-given though she did not know it initially. But in 1996, when God called her into fulltime ministry, one of the first things He said was that He was giving her a writing ministry. So her natural talents and desires were actually strong pointers to the purpose of God for her life. Today, she heads our church's publishing ministry.

Friend, what do you desire to become in life? Have you noticed that you have a particular passion or desire for something? Pursue it! But make sure that your desire is not birthed out of jealousy, pride, covetousness, or any sinful attitudes. If your desire is rooted in a genuine passion to bring glory to God, you will excel.

Often, your desires are expressed in the dreams or visions you have for your life. We live in a dreamer's world. Every great invention or outstanding accomplishment is born of a dream. A wise man once said, "Show me a dreamer, and I will show you a man to behold."

When I'm talking about dreaming, I'm not talking about having a balloon imagination in the middle of the night. I am talking about visualizing a glorious tomorrow with absolute confidence. I am talking about visualizing a destination that is born out of knowledge, passion, or an encounter with God.

Dr. David Yonggi Cho, the pastor of the world's largest congregation, once said that visions and dreams are the language of the Holy Spirit. A person can never amount to any more than what they dream of being. In short, you cannot grow or prosper beyond your dream. So if you desire greatness, dream great dreams! Dr. Cho knows this firsthand. He is a man who knows how to dream big. The result of his grand dreams has been great accomplishments. The most outstanding is his phenomenally large megachurch of 780,000 registered members!

KEEP ON DREAMING!

To be dreamless in a dreamer's world is to be doomed. If you want to press into the glorious future that God has in store for you, you must forever be a visionary. There must never be a time when you do not have a God-given dream to pursue.

I believe the reason why many people, especially Christians, die so young these days has nothing to do with physical illness. It has to do with the fact that they have stopped dreaming. I once heard of a great man of God who was fond of saying, "There's nothing that God has told me to do that I haven't done. I've done everything; I've done everything." Well, this man died prematurely, and I believe his untimely death had a lot to do with the fact that he had no more dreams left to accomplish.

If you're satisfied with where you are in life today, you'll never go forward. But if you say, "Thank God for where I am today, but I need to press forward to greater things," God will propel you forward. Don't be too satisfied or comfortable with where you are now. Do not rest in yesterday's glories, either. Target a more glorious future. Keep on moving on!

Millionaire Joshua spent his life conquering and claiming the land that God had promised His people, the Israelites. Yet in his old age, God visited him one day with a wake-up call. The Lord said to him, *"You are old, advanced in years, and there remains very much land yet to be possessed"* (Joshua 13:1).

God was plainly telling Joshua, "Yes, you have accomplished much, but there is still much more that you can do. *There remains very much land yet to be possessed.*" In essence, He was saying, *"Joshua, do not even think of retirement. Do not stop dreaming. If you stop dreaming, you will stop achieving!"*

Keep in mind that at the time God was speaking to Joshua, he was old and advanced in years. Many people feel that only young people can dream. As far as God is concerned, old age should not stop you from dreaming or achieving. This is why He says in Joel 2:28, *"And it shall come to pass afterward, that I will pour out My Spirit on all flesh.... Your old men shall dream dreams."*

Millionaire Abraham was not a young man when God gave him his dream. He was an old man of seventy-five years. No matter how old you are, regardless of the success that you have enjoyed in life, there's always much more to be done or accomplished. Never settle for the status quo. Move beyond your present level, and keep dreaming of a greater and better future. You need to keep on moving, going higher, and growing!

Having big dreams concerning your financial freedom is the starting point of achieving them. When your dream of becoming a Bible-made millionaire is grounded in a genuine desire to add value to humanity, God will help you.

Beloved, every dreamer naturally ends up as a ruler. The Bible-made millionaires of old did not live lives of chance. They lived lives of purpose. They knew the path that God had ordained for them in life and followed it faithfully. Hence, they prospered exceedingly.

Everyone who wishes to become a Bible-made millionaire must create a clear vision, or dream, of financial success and freedom. The clearer your vision of wealth and prosperity, the faster you will move toward it, and the faster it will move toward you. Remember this universal law of attraction: Whatever you want wants you! When you desire wealth for God's kingdom purpose, God's kingdom wealth will gravitate toward you.

Chapter 5

Secret #3: Create Strategies to Make Your Purpose a Reality

> Any enterprise is built by wise planning, becomes strong through common sense, and profits wonderfully by keeping abreast of the facts.
>
> Proverbs 24:3-4, TLB

Nothing just happens automatically on its own. No vision is self- fulfilling. *Every purpose birthed in the heart of man becomes accomplished through deliberate steps of action.*

Bible-made millionaires are not just visionaries. They are also wise, creative planners who embrace the right strategies needed to make their dreams a reality. It is one thing for you to talk about becoming a millionaire; it's another thing for you to actually take the necessary steps required to achieve millionaire status. If you want to achieve financial success, you must do something—not just *anything*, but the *right things* needed to achieve your goal.

In order to grow financially from where you are today to where you want to be tomorrow, you need to understand and implement wise biblical strategies. Remember: *Any enterprise is build by wise planning, and profits wonderfully by keeping abreast of the facts* (Proverbs 24:3-4, TLB).

Flourishing enterprises, successful careers, and financial empires do not just spring up out of the blue. *They are built by wise planning.* If you desire to become a millionaire, don't just talk the talk. You must also walk the walk! You must have a clear plan of action by which you will carry out your purpose each and every day that you wake up.

There are five key biblical strategies that every believer must follow to turn their dream of becoming a Bible-made millionaire into a reality. These lines of action will help establish and keep you on the course of financial success throughout your journey in life. I have seen these principles work in my personal life and ministry. Friend, if you embrace these plans, in due season, you will become a Bible-made millionaire. God's Word can never fail, and it will never return back to Him void.

1. Break Down Your Purpose Into Clearly Defined Goals.

> A man's heart plans his way, But the LORD directs his steps.
>
> Proverbs 16:9

A *step* is a stage in the fulfillment of a plan. It is one of a series of actions or measures taken to achieve a desired goal. It is the ongoing pursuit of a worthy objective until it is accomplished.

God divides every dream or plan that He births in the heart of man into single steps or goals. No matter how big and grand the dream that He gives you, understand that He never intends for you to accomplish it in one giant leap. Instead, He wants it to be fulfilled, or established, step by step.

> The **steps** of a good man are ordered by the LORD, And He delights in his way.
>
> Psalm 37:23

> "For precept must be upon precept, precept upon precept, Line upon line, line upon line, Here a little, there a little."
>
> Isaiah 28:10

Therefore, to fulfill your vision, you must break it down into simple clear-cut steps, or achievable goals. Goals help translate your dream from the realm of the intangible to the tangible; from concept to reality. No dream can be accomplished by impulsive or unstructured actions. Clear- cut short- and long-term goals all add up to the overall fulfillment of your purpose and the realization of your financial dreams.

It is unrealistic to attempt to fulfill your purpose without a well-defined plan of action. Impractical people attend one how-to-become-a-millionaire seminar after the other, yet they never take any definitive action toward making their dream a reality because they fail to set goals for themselves. To become a Bible-made millionaire, you must set goals for your life and passionately pursue them to completion.

There are five key factors to consider when you are breaking your dream down into goals.

Five Steps to Successful Goal Setting

A. Decide exactly what you want to accomplish.

Goal setting begins by first knowing exactly what it is you want to accomplish. You must have a clear picture in your mind of your mission. What are you living for? What is your passion? Do not be vague. Be specific.

One of the richest men in U.S. history, the famous oil billionaire H. L. Hunt was once asked his formula for success. His response was to know what you want, and to be ready to pay the price to achieve it.

If you aim at everything, you will achieve nothing! If you do not know precisely what you want to achieve, you will keep going round and round in circles. You must mark your target and embrace what it takes to reach it. Specifically decide a worthy cause to live for, so that your life is defined and driven by it each day.

B. Clearly and specifically write down your goals.

> Then the LORD answered me and said: "Write the vision And make it plain on tablets, That he may run who reads it."
>
> Habakkuk 2:2

A goal that is not written down is merely a wish or a fantasy. If God has birthed a vision in your heart, it is your duty to write it down in clear, specific terms. Make it plain. Writing energizes your goals. It prompts immediate action on the part of the reader; it compels him to run!

This, in turn, leads to the ultimate fulfillment of the dream. On the other hand, an unwritten dream lacks the energy needed for movement. It cannot preempt action. Simply put, if the vision is not written down, no one can run to fulfill it.

Researchers claim that only 3 percent of the population actually puts their goals in writing. The other 97 percent, who don't, merely have wishes, hopes, and fantasies. They cannot be said to have goals.

People without written goals are doomed to a lifetime of working for those who do have clearly defined and written goals. Zig Ziglar, the great motivational speaker, says that written goals transform you from a wandering generality into a meaningful specific. Take your vision beyond the realm of fantasy. Write down your God-given dream so that *you may run when you read it.*

C. Set a deadline for your goal, and sub-deadlines, if necessary.

After you have clearly written down your goal, you must proceed to set a deadline for its fulfillment. Do not just have clearly written goals; also have clearly defined timeframes in which you intend for your goal to be accomplished. For instance, if your goal is to increase your income or profits, define specifically how much more money you would like to make and within what specified timeframe.

Unless you attach a set time to your goal, procrastination, which is a thief of destiny, will set in. Instead of advancing toward the fulfillment of your goal, you will keep postponing what you should do now to a more "convenient" time, until eventually it never gets done.

Procrastination will hamper your progress in your quest for success. To avoid falling into its trap, you must set definite deadlines for your goals. This will instill in you the sense of urgency that you need to successfully pursue your dream. When you operate on a deadline, you'll understand that you do not have the luxury of time on your side. You will use your time wisely, redeeming every second of it for your task.

When you realize that you are accountable to perform and "deliver" at the scheduled time, you'll maximize your time and creative energies to accomplish your purpose within the set timeframe. In this regard, deadlines help release your creative juices and propel you to do whatever it takes to achieve your purpose. Without deadlines, you will be lax and not feel compelled to act or think progressively.

D. MAKE A LIST OF EVERYTHING YOU HAVE TO DO TO ACHIEVE YOUR GOAL.

A daily or weekly planner is an indispensable tool for the Bible-made millionaire. It is a little notebook in which you outline the daily program or activities in which your goals will be carried out on a continual basis.

It is not enough to have a clearly written goal. You must also write down, daily or weekly, the concrete action steps that must be executed to achieve that goal. Every day of your life must move you further along in the fulfillment of your purpose. Daily movement toward your goal will energize you and increase your confidence.

Once you know exactly what you need to do with your time, prioritize and sequence the steps in your plan. Rework your plan as needed until you accomplish your aim.

E. TAKE ACTION ON YOUR PLAN IMMEDIATELY.

Resolve to do something every day that moves you toward your goal. If you perform just one task in your planner each day, no matter how insurmountable that goal appears to be or how far away it may seem, this single action will keep you motivated and focused.

Many people fail to accomplish their goals because they don't take immediate action on their plans. Do not postpone to a more convenient time what you ought to do today. Remember, procrastination is a thief of destiny. It denies great dreams and visions from becoming reality.

The discipline of doing something every day enables you to develop and maintain momentum. So do something every day to move you in the direction of your goals. Act as though the achievement of your goal is inevitable, and adopt a mentality that in your quest for success, failure is not an option!

Benjamin Franklin, America's first millionaire, once said that he started each day with the following question: "What do I want to accomplish today?" He wrote it down. At the end of the day before he went to bed, he asked the follow-up question: "What have you achieved today?"

Mary Kay, the founder of Mary Kay Cosmetics, would also start each day by writing down six things on her to-do list for the day. Before she retired to bed, she would review her list and assess her progress. Her structured life played a large role in the phenomenal success of Mary Kay Cosmetics, a company she founded in 1963 with her life savings of $5,000, but which today has grown into a multi-billion-dollar worldwide thriving enterprise.

Millionaires live very ordered lives. They don't spend their time frivolously. They invest their time wisely. They make each second of their life count for something. They are constantly asking themselves, "What have I done today to move closer to my goals?"

2. GIVE YOURSELF TO HARD WORK.

> Do you see a man who excels in his work? He will stand before kings; He will not stand before unknown men.
>
> Proverbs 22:29

> The hand of the diligent will rule, But the lazy man will be put to forced labor.
>
> Proverbs 12:24

Do what you love with passion and excellence, and you will experience great financial success. If you focus on what you do best and strive to be a leader in your field of expertise, money will follow you. The word *excel* is also translated to mean "diligent."

A man who is diligent and works hard in everything he does will stand before nobility and greatness. He will never find himself in the company of mediocrity. In your journey to becoming a Bible-made millionaire, you must embrace a strong work ethic. God will never prosper a lazy man. You can dream and talk about prosperity all you want, but if you are not prepared to engage in the virtue of hard work, your talk and desires will amount to nothing.

> In all labor there is profit, But idle chatter leads only to poverty.
>
> Proverbs 14:23

God is committed by covenant to prosper everyone who walks uprightly before Him. Psalm 1:1-3 says:

> Blessed is the man Who walks not in the counsel of the ungodly, Nor stands in the path of sinners, Nor sits in the seat of the scornful; But his delight is in the law of the LORD, And in His law he meditates day and night. He shall be like a tree Planted by the rivers of water, That brings forth its fruit in its season, Whose leaf also shall not wither; **And whatever he does shall prosper** (emphasis mine).

Yet as much as God wants you to prosper, He can only prosper what you do. *He cannot prosper what you do not do!* He cannot prosper your inactivity!

No matter how righteous you are, if you are idle, God cannot prosper you. The key words in these scriptures are "*whatever he does.*" These mean work! God can't bless wishful thinking. He cannot bless laziness. He can only bless what you do, that is, your work.

Anything of value doesn't come cheap. *Every prize has a price*. The price for prosperity is hard work. The price for profit is labor. Remember, *"In all labor there is profit...."* The Bible-made millionaires of old understood this infallible principle, and as such, they were very hard workers. They became millionaires as a result of their tireless and creative labor.

Millionaire Abraham was a hard-working husbandman who diligently tended his herds. If he were not a worker, God would have had nothing to bless. Remember, God blesses work, not wishful thinking.

Millionaire Jacob, Abraham's grandson, had virtually nothing when he arrived at his Uncle Laban's house. Though he was cheated and treated very poorly by his employer, through hard work and creativity, he was able to turn his almost twenty years of menial labor into great wealth and prosperity. Jacob put his creative mind to work, effectively managing the flock in Laban's house to the point that he became even wealthier than his employer!

> But when the flocks were feeble, he did not put them in; **so the feebler were Laban's and the stronger Jacob's. Thus the man became exceedingly prosperous, and had large flocks, female and male servants, and camels and donkeys.**
>
> Genesis 30:42-43, emphasis mine

Millionaire Solomon was not just a man of wisdom. He was also a hard worker. Solomon didn't become rich solely because God gave him wisdom. No doubt, wisdom was a part of his secret to success. However, without work, his wisdom would have left Solomon a wise pauper! Ecclesiastes 9:15 makes us understand that there are some people who are wise, yet poor.

> Now there was found in it a poor wise man, and he by his wisdom delivered the city. Yet no one remembered that same poor man.

Typically, it is abnormal for a wise man to be poor. Wisdom brings riches, not poverty: *Length of days is in her right hand, in her left hand riches and honor* (Proverbs 3:16). Riches and honor go together with wisdom, enduring riches, and righteousness (see Proverbs 8:18). However, wise men may remain poor if they fail to engage in a strong work ethic.

It is one thing for you to have wisdom; it's yet another thing to put your wisdom to use in order for it to work for you. It is not possible for you to possess the wisdom of God, put it to work, and still remain poor. When you add hard work to your God-given wisdom, you will surely excel.

Millionaire Solomon learned early in his reign that though God had endowed him with wisdom, he still had to do his part. He had to work hard. Solomon understood that it was his labor, not wisdom alone, that would cause him to profit and experience the unprecedented fame, wealth, and prestige that God had promised him.

> I made my works great, I built myself houses, and planted myself vineyards. I made myself gardens and orchards, and I planted all kinds of fruit trees in them. I made myself water pools from which to water the growing trees of the

> grove. I acquired male and female servants, and had servants born in my house. Yes, I had greater possessions of herds and flocks than all who were in Jerusalem before me. I also gathered for myself silver and gold and the special treasures of kings and of the provinces. I acquired male and female singers, the delights of the sons of men, and musical instruments of all kinds.
> So I became great and excelled more than all who were before me in Jerusalem. Also my wisdom remained with me. Whatever my eyes desired I did not keep from them. I did not withhold my heart from any pleasure, For my heart rejoiced in all my labor; And this was my reward from all my labor.
>
> Ecclesiastes 2:4-10

Solomon became a man of wealth by making his work great, and he rejoiced in all his labor. He did not grumble at labor. He rejoiced and was happy to work. He was a multi-billionaire as a result of the works of his hands, which God blessed and prospered. Understand that the desire to succeed in life or at any venture is not enough. You must also be ready to take action and work toward the fulfillment of your dream.

What about Millionaire Uzziah, the great-great-grandson of Solomon? Uzziah became a great king, builder, innovator, and an inventor largely because he worked tirelessly. He took the deliveries of God's blessings and promises by his labor.

> And Uzziah built towers in Jerusalem at the Corner Gate, at the Valley Gate, and at the corner buttress of the wall; then he fortified them. Also

> he built towers in the desert. He dug many wells, for he had much livestock, both in the lowlands and in the plains; he also had farmers and vinedressers in the mountains and in Carmel, for he loved the soil. Moreover Uzziah had an army of fighting men who went out to war by companies, according to the number on their roll as prepared by Jeiel the scribe and Maaseiah the officer, under the hand of Hananiah, one of the king's captains. The total number of chief officers of the mighty men of valor was two thousand six hundred. And under their authority was an army of three hundred and seven thousand five hundred, that made war with mighty power, to help the king against the enemy. Then Uzziah prepared for them, for the entire army, shields, spears, helmets, body armor, bows, and slings to cast stones. And he made devices in Jerusalem, invented by skillful men, to be on the towers and the corners, to shoot arrows and large stones. So his fame spread far and wide, for he was marvelously helped till he became strong.
>
> 2 Chronicles 26:9-15

Even the Lord Jesus had to work hard during His three-year ministry on earth. He was mightily anointed, but He was also a very hard worker. His work caused Him to prosper and be distinguished in His earthly assignment.

> "I must work the works of Him who sent Me while it is day; the night is coming when no one can work."
>
> John 9:4

> But Jesus answered them, "My Father has been working until now, and I have been working."
>
> John 5:17

God wants to prosper everything you do. However, if you're not working, God has nothing to prosper. So do not just dream, take action. Work!

> The soul of a lazy man desires, and has nothing;
> But the soul of the diligent shall be made rich.
>
> Proverbs 13:4

This also means that you should work hard at improving your skills. The fastest way to get rich, grow rich, and stay rich is to work on developing yourself through formal or informal training.

Wealthy American industrialist J. Paul Getty once said that the man who comes up with a means for doing or producing almost anything better, faster, or more economically has his future and his fortune at his fingertips. When you study hard to become an expert at what you are doing, you will never be ashamed. *Instead you will be acclaimed!* (See 2 Timothy 2:15.)

You may be talented and you may have the grace of God upon your life, but if you are not a hard worker, that anointing or grace will be in vain. The Apostle Paul is considered to be the mightiest apostle in the Bible. What distinguished Paul from the other apostles? Hard work! He wrote more than half of the New Testament because of his commitment to hard work. He understood the dignity of labor. He was a tireless worker for the kingdom of God. In 1 Corinthians 15:10, Paul said:

> But by the grace of God I am what I am, and His grace toward me was not in vain; but I labored more abundantly than they all, yet not I, but the grace of God which was with me.

Paul became a mighty apostle through the dignity of labor. Brethren, in whatever we do, we are commanded to work hard at it and do it excellently. This way we can never escape God's prosperity.

Today, many people in the world complain of racism as a barrier to their success. I am not denying that racism exists. However, I strongly believe that diligent work and excellence in the workplace is one of the greatest deterrents to racism. No matter what your color is, if you do your job diligently and better than anyone else, you will stand out. People will respect you.

My father-in-law had an interesting experience while working in the United States in the 1970s. His boss was a man who always went home and spoke excitedly about Daddy's exceptional performance on the job to his wife. His boss, however, never mentioned that this brilliant worker was an African. One day, Dad was invited to a company function where his boss and his wife were also in attendance. His boss was glad that he finally had the opportunity to introduce his favorite team member to his wife. However, her first reaction to her husband's introduction to Dad was not one of excitement. On the contrary, she was so shocked to discover that his highly prized employee was a black man that she fainted!

Not in a million years would she have thought that the man her husband had been raving about all these years was an African. She said that she had never expected that that type of brilliance and diligence could ever come from the black race. Dad, through hard work and excellence, stood out and gained the respect of his white boss during an era of intense racial discrimination.

When you give yourself to hard work and excellence, prejudiced, narrow-minded people may faint because of you! But, as for you, you will never be fired! You will keep excelling marvelously in all your endeavors. Even if people don't like you because of the color of your skin, companies and supervisors will always place the highest value on excellence that leads to improved productivity.

Friend, nothing works until you work it out. Make no mistake about it: The key to living out your dream of becoming a Bible-made millionaire is in working out your plan. Do what God has assigned you to do with all your might.

Some people are too casual with their calling. Only the diligent will prosper and stand out in life. If you're a diligent worker, you stand to gain the best that God has promised you. Hard work will not kill you. It'll only make you shine!

3. Give Yourself to Qualitative Thinking.

> For as he thinks in his heart, so is he.
>
> Proverbs 23:7a

Your mentality is one of the greatest molders of destiny. You cannot rise beyond the quality of your thoughts. You can only go as far in life as your mind can conceive. Therefore, your mind is one of your greatest assets. Whatever your mind cannot see, your physical eyes cannot see, either. So you need to think qualitatively if you want to enjoy a life of prosperity.

The wonders and wealth we see in the universe today are products of God's wise and creative thinking. Proverbs 3:19-20 says:

> The LORD by wisdom founded the earth; By understanding He established the heavens; By His knowledge the depths were broken up, And clouds drop down the dew.

> O LORD, how manifold are thy works! in wisdom hast thou made them all: the earth is full of thy riches.
>
> Psalm 104:24, KJV

Just as God's works are a product of His thoughts, so also your works should be products of your thoughts. Great thinking produces great treasures. They produce great destinies.

As a believer, you have the ability to think qualitatively because you have the mind of Christ. First Corinthians 2:16 says, *For who has known the mind of the Lord that he may instruct Him? But we have the mind of Christ.*

You must engage the mind of Christ, which you have, in creative thought to establish every good purpose that God has birthed in your heart. No matter how great your vision or dream is, you need wise thinking to accomplish it. The extent to which you engage in productive thinking will determine the extent to which you will prosper in life.

Every transformation of life takes root in the mind. There can't be a breakthrough in your financial future, profession, business enterprise, or home unless you first have a breakthrough in your thinking. The level to which you engage your mind in productive thought will determine the level of results you'll obtain in your endeavors. If you can engage your mind in qualitative thinking, you're going to have outstanding results. *A breakthrough in your mind equals a breakthrough in your life!*

By the power of your God-given mind, you can innovate and birth new things. You carry a creative ability on the inside of you, so make use of your mind to create new things. Your mind is the seat of image formation. Through the power of your imagination, you can form images in your mind that will motivate you to great accomplishments. Imagination creates zeal for performance. With your creative mind, you do not need to wait for things to happen. *You can make things happen.*

So your mind is not just a bank of information alone, but a huge storage of energy that keeps you moving toward your goal. When you engage your mind in a productive way, you will have good results. When you become a thinker, life will begin to deliver its best for you. This is because *you cannot be creative without being productive, and you cannot be productive without being financially successful.*

One of the greatest pitfalls of religion is what I call *mental paralysis*. Many Christians have actually abandoned the role of qualitative thinking in their faith. They think that as long as they pray, they don't have to think. Friend, remember that there's nothing in existence today that does not have the force of a qualitative mind behind it.

Beloved, not every problem in life is from the devil. Some problems come as a result of a lack of qualitative thinking. Many believers today don't have a money problem. They have a wisdom or thinking, problem! They do not have a problem of lack. Rather they lack the wise idea that will bring abundance into their lives.

There are some people who claim to think, yet they do not think right thoughts. They think retrogressively instead of progressively. Instead of dreaming of a glorious future, they dwell on the negatives of the past. Remember, you can never rise above the level of your thoughts—as a man thinks in his heart, so is he. God expects you to use the mind of Christ, which He has given you, to think forward, not backward. Think your way out of poverty, lack, and despair.

We see the life-changing power of qualitative thinking at work in the story of the Prodigal Son in Luke 15. It is the story of a son who rejects his father's guidance. Prideful and self-confident, he heads off to a faraway land, leads a wild life of adventure, and squanders his precious inheritance. Not until he's confronted with failure and despair does he return home, repentant and willing to do anything to win back his father's favor. To his surprise, he's welcomed back into his father's loving and forgiving arms. He is also restored to the honor and dignity that he had lost.

But what prompted the cycle of positive change in the prodigal's life? The answer is found in Luke 15:17-18a (emphasis mine).

> "But **when he came to himself**, he said, 'How many of my father's hired servants have bread enough and to spare, and I perish with hunger! **I will arise** and go to my father…'"

Change began when the prodigal "came to himself," when he started thinking qualitatively! When he began to think progressively, he was motivated to arise—to stand up from his pit of despair and move on to better things.

Qualitative thinking is progressive. It is never retrogressive. It will always compel you to move forward, never backward. It is impossible for you to go backward in life when you engage your mind in creative thought. No matter how many mistakes you have made in the past, you have the power to change your direction for the best if you will begin to think qualitatively. Remember, change in your circumstances first begins with a change in your mind.

In your glorious mind lies the answer to the issues of your life. Proverbs 20:5 says, *Counsel in the heart of man is like deep water, but a man of understanding will draw it out.* Think deeply, meditating on God's Word, and you will find the wisdom that God has provided to solve questions such as, "How do I take this business enterprise to the next level?" or, "How can I increase my income?" Anytime you engage your mind in qualitative thinking, you will get a divinely inspired idea, which can create wealth for you.

Friend, men of ideas rule the world! When you engage your mind in qualitative thought, you will always be on top. You will reign victoriously and prosperously in life. People who do not think qualitatively will always work for those who do. God has given you the mind of Jesus for you to be above only, never beneath—always producing wealth-generating ideas that bring glory to God and deliver blessings to mankind!

4. Associate with People of Purpose.

After the Lord reveals your purpose to you in prayer, one of the first things you should do is to sit at the feet of others who have done what God is calling you to do and learn how they've done it.

The truth is, there is no such thing as a self-made person. Every successful person is the product of his predecessors. The great scientist Sir Isaac Newton once said, "If I have seen farther than others it is because I have climbed on the shoulders of those who have gone ahead of me."

Ecclesiastes 1:9-10 says, *That which has been is what will be, that which is done is what will be done, and there is nothing new under the sun. Is there anything of which it may be said, "See, this is new"? It has already been in ancient times before us.*

Indeed, there is nothing new under the sun. In the truest sense of the word, there is no new invention or business in the world. There are only better ways of doing what has already existed before. Every so-called invention or innovation is actually an improvement on what *already has been in ancient times.*

Whatever it is you desire to do, whether it is pursuing a particular career or opening a specific kind of business, never forget that what you are planning to do is not really new. There are others who have gone ahead of you and have done exactly what you are planning to do. If you desire to excel even more than they did, the wise thing to do is to learn from their example. As Sir Isaac Newton said, "*Climb on their shoulders.*" Then you will see farther than they ever did, and get greater results than they ever had. If you have the opportunity, develop close relationships with them. You will benefit a great deal from their mentorship. You will learn to avoid the mistakes that they made and adopt their winning strategies.

Never isolate yourself from your predecessors. Those who walk in isolation will never make a mark in this life. Joining yourself with achievers who have gone ahead of you is one of the surest strategies to successfully accomplishing your dreams. Millionaire Isaac prospered because of his close association to his father, Millionaire Abraham. This was also true of Millionaire Solomon. He prospered above all the kings of the earth because he stood on the shoulders of his father, David. He did not isolate himself from him.

Before Dominion International Center was inaugurated, I took time to learn at the feet of the experts. I traveled out of the country to consult with mentors and make inquiries of them. I also read biographies of many men of God who had already done what I was trying to do, and I learned what they had done and how they had done it.

Successful people are not different from anyone else. If you do what they are doing, you will get the same results! So never be too proud to ask for help. You can always learn something from those who are farther down the road than you are. Yoke yourself to people who are financially successful. Learn what they have done to be successful. Understand their mistakes so you don't have to make them yourself. Align yourself with those who can help you, and learn at their feet. In due season, the milk and honey of the land … great wealth … will start flowing to you, too!

5. Make God Your CEO.

Bible-made millionaires do not just love God and embrace His ways, they also seek His wisdom in the way they conduct their enterprise or endeavors. They esteem Him as their Chief Executive Officer.

They understand that God is the real Owner of their business or careers. He is their Employer; they are merely His employees. As a result, they acknowledge Him in all their ways. They do not do anything without consulting with Him. They seek and rely on God's counsel alone in all things. They choose His wisdom above their own. Bible-made millionaires do not make any decision without consulting God first. Why? Because the Bible says:

> Trust in the LORD with all your heart, And lean not on your own understanding; In all your ways acknowledge Him, And He shall direct your paths. Do not be wise in your own eyes. Fear the LORD and depart from evil.
>
> Proverbs 3:5-7

When you esteem God as your CEO, your business will become God's full responsibility. It is no longer your business; it is His. And He will personally shoulder everything that concerns the business. Whatever battle the company faces will not be your battle; it will be God's battle. In the most turbulent financial climate, God will be with you and see you through. He says in Isaiah 43:2:

> When you pass through the waters, I will be with you; And through the rivers, they shall not overflow you. When you walk through the fire, you shall not be burned, Nor shall the flame scorch you.

Not only will God deliver you from trouble, as your CEO, He will enlarge and expand your business. He will build your career in a way you never could. Perhaps you've been handling your business or profession on your own. It's time to give God full control. Surrender it all to Him. Let His supreme wisdom take you to the highest level of success and prosperity!

Having God as our CEO has been the secret of our success at Dominion International Center. I've not been the pastor of DIC for one day. No! I am just an under shepherd. God is the true Pastor and Shepherd of our church. I am just a member like everyone else.

You will never hear me refer to DIC as "my church," because it's not! If it were my church, I would carry all of its challenges upon my shoulders; I would not be able to rest well at night. At DIC, we have given God full responsibility for our church. He fights our battles. He commands our breakthroughs. Since it is God's church and not mine, I sleep like a baby every night because the Lord says, "I will build My church." It is God's duty to build; it is mine only to obey Him.

Please catch this revelation: Your business is not *your business*. It is God's business! Give Him the ownership. Let Him be the Owner, for He is the best Businessman ever. With Him at the helm, your business, your company, your career will never be misguided! It will never go down; it will only go up. It will continue to prosper exceedingly because He *is "the LORD your God, who teaches you to profit, who leads you by the way you should go"* (Isaiah 48:17). Align yourself with God, and He will tell you exactly what you need to do to go to the next level of prosperity.

In February 1992, a precious sister and member of the church that I was pastoring at the time came to me complaining of how unprofitable her business was. As she was speaking, the Holy Spirit spoke to my heart concerning her situation. He revealed to me that this lady had been the chairman, owner, and all in all of her business. He, the Lord, had been relegated to the background. He told me that if she wanted to begin to see profits in her business, she must give God full control of it. God had to become the Chairman of her business if it was to experience His blessing.

He told me to tell her to seek God's counsel in everything that concerned her business. Specifically, God also told her to obey whatever instruction God gave regarding the profits that she would make. She embraced my God-given counsel. And sure enough, her business began to prosper. In accordance with God's instruction, she did not consider the business profits to be hers. Rather, she esteemed them as the Lord's and hence sought direction from God about what to do with the profits. The Lord instructed her to give, as an offering, approximately 75 percent of the profits. She obeyed God without question and made out a check to the church.

Her business continued to prosper remarkably. And when she made a profit on a second contract, she did not hesitate to inquire of the Lord what to do with it. This time He said, "You keep 50 percent of the profits and bring 50 percent to Me." She obeyed.

A while after that, she had a great financial quarter, which ended with triple the profits she had recorded previously. This time God's instruction was, "Everything is Mine." Staying true to her commitment to keep God as her company's CEO, she obeyed and gave it all, as a charitable donation, sacrificially to the Lord. After all, it was God's company, not hers. She was just His employee.

Her continued obedience caused God to elevate her once-struggling company to an astronomical success. A few months after she recorded her 300-percent increase in profits, she landed a huge contract that raked in profits twenty-five times more than she had ever made!

Again she went to God, her CEO, and inquired about how to apply the profits. To which God responded, "Just pay your tithes and keep the rest for yourself." This time God said, "Just give Me 10 percent and spend the remaining 90 percent as you choose." Her company, her financial status, experienced a radical turn, all because she made God her CEO!

A year later, her face beaming with joy, she excitedly testified to me that she had now become a millionaire. In such a short period, through faithful obedience to the instruction of her CEO, she had bounced back from the brink of economic disaster to incredible financial bloom!

Without God, it is impossible to reach your goals of financial prosperity. It is the help of God that facilitates the strategies, the plans, and the relationships that need to be in place to make your goals a reality. When you give God His place in your life, you secure your own place of honor. Remember the words of Matthew 6:33: *"But seek first the kingdom of God and His righteousness, and all these things shall be added to you."*

Until you give God the preeminence in your life, the fulfillment of your dreams is uncertain, and your dreaming will degenerate to mere daydreaming.

Every progress in life is made by the help of God's Holy Spirit. Where you place God in your heart determines where you end up in life. If the status you desire in life, be it financial or otherwise, does not exalt God, He will not help you get there. Where God will not be glorified, He will never show up. But you can count on God's help and leading when you esteem Him as the Most High, giving Him all the glory in all your endeavors.

Chapter 6

Secret #4: Make Integrity Your Watchword

> For the upright shall dwell in the land, and the men of integrity, blameless and complete [in God's sight], shall remain in it.
>
> Proverbs 2:21, AMP

Integrity is the quality or state of being upright, honest, and sincere. It is having sound moral principles. A man of integrity is one whose words match his deeds. His reputation is solid, and his dealings are straightforward. In this sense, integrity has a lot to do with keeping your word and being true to your agreements.

Integrity is a quality that is seriously lacking in today's society. Sadly, this is true even in the Christian community. You simply cannot count on the word of some believers. They may profess one thing, yet they do another. They refuse to fulfill promises or obligations; they do not treat deadlines seriously and always come up with excuses for failure. Such people cannot go far in life. They cannot enjoy millionaire status, either, because *integrity and uprightness are preservers of destiny.*

Today, in the quest for wealth, many have relegated honor and truth to the background. But you must understand that God is a God of integrity, and He desires you to be like that, too. Everything that God does, He does in integrity and truth.

> For the word of the LORD is right, And all His work is done in truth. He loves righteousness and justice; The earth is full of the goodness of the LORD.
>
> Psalm 33:4-5

God wants you to perform all your works like Him—your business, your endeavors, your enterprises—in sincerity, honesty, and truth. God commanded Millionaire Solomon to walk in integrity that his throne might be prolonged.

> "Now if you walk before Me as your father David walked, in integrity of heart and in uprightness, to do according to all that I have commanded you, and if you keep My statutes and My judgments, then I will establish the throne of your kingdom over Israel forever, as I promised David your father, saying, 'You shall not fail to have a man on the throne of Israel.'"
>
> 1 King 9:4-5

To secure the financial throne that God has ordained for you, to enjoy the wealth that He has stored up for you, you must make integrity your watchword. It is the hallmark of true and lasting riches.

Your integrity will enthrone you, but a lack of integrity will cause anyone to lose his throne. Any wealth amassed outside of integrity will not last. Wealth gained by dishonesty, deception, or corruption will surely, without a doubt, be diminished.

> Wealth gained by dishonesty will be diminished,
> But he who gathers by labor will increase.
>
> Proverbs 13:11

In any organization where the leaders lack integrity, that organization, no matter how big, won't last. The tragic fall of Enron, once the seventh largest corporation in the U.S., is a typical example of this. Established in 1985 by Ken Lay, at its peak Enron was worth about $70 billion and its shares traded for about $90. However, what was once a thriving company declared bankruptcy on December 2, 2001. Enron's catastrophic fall is largely blamed on the fraudulent practices of its high- ranking officials. Charges against Enron's top executives ranged from money laundering to lying to investors about the company's financial health. These malpractices led to the massive job loss of thousands of Enron employees. Moreover, thousands of investors, mostly Enron employees, also lost billions of dollars in investments as the Enron stock fell drastically. The Enron scandal is said to have been one of the biggest corporate frauds in history. Its fall testifies to the fact that where integrity is lacking, success cannot be sustained.

If you desire to be a Bible-made millionaire, you must embrace integrity from the start! Do not build your business or career on crookedness. Top priority must be given to your character development if you want to achieve millionaire status the Bible way. Moreover, if you own a business, it is your responsibility to instill and demand integrity from your employees. Any employee who lacks integrity may be the undoing of that company, even if the leadership is sound.

You can stand out and excel in life simply by committing yourself to live strictly by God's righteous, moral codes. Wealth and riches will forever remain in the house of the upright, or the man of integrity.

> The Lord knows the days of the upright, And their inheritance shall be forever.
>
> Psalm 37:18

Conversely, a sinful and decadent lifestyle brings downfall and demotion to any person or business. Proverbs 14:34 says, *Righteousness exalts a nation, but sin is a reproach to any people.*

Only the upright will enjoy God's backing in the race of success. If you desire to be a Bible-made millionaire, you must take the matter of integrity very seriously. God will never help a dishonest or corrupt person to prosper. You need integrity both to attain your wealth and to sustain it. Integrity will not only secure a great financial future for you, but it will also secure a future for your children for years to come. It is a producer of blessings that continue on throughout the generations. This is why the issue of integrity matters a lot to Bible-made millionaires.

> The righteous man walks in his integrity; His children are blessed after him.
>
> Proverbs 20:7

> The house of the wicked will be overthrown, But the tent of the upright will flourish.
>
> Proverbs 14:11

Remember, a Bible-made millionaire is not just someone who is wealthy. He is a person who has acquired his riches by God's power and for God's purpose. His riches are as a result of God's enabling, not human engineering. Therefore, Bible-made millionaires understand that in order to enjoy God's backing where their finances are concerned, they must fully embrace His standards of living and conduct all their affairs in honesty.

There are many today who would rather go for *fame* than a *good name.* They give no regard to integrity in their quest for wealth and prominence. They would do literally anything for money and power. Corruption and malpractice are not only common in our modern-day business world, but to a certain degree, it has even become acceptable. The popular philosophy of many is: *The means justifies the end.* Simply put, they say, "*It does not matter what you do to get results, as long as you get them.*"

But it is different in God's world. He places a higher value on integrity than on riches. Proverbs 22:1 says, *A good name is to be chosen rather than great riches, loving favor rather than silver and gold.* In God's kingdom, how you acquire your wealth is more important than wealth itself. This does not mean that you should lose your desire to prosper. But it means that you should make up your mind that *you will not sacrifice your integrity for the sake of prosperity.* As an aspiring Bible-made millionaire, you must realize that it is more important to be known as a person of integrity than to be known as a person of wealth. You must be more interested in *maintaining a good reputation* than in *making money*.

Wealth gained through crooked means will never be justified or endorsed by God. Wealth gained through corruption and dishonesty is cursed of the Lord, and it will eventually bring pain and shame to those involved. As a result, He expects you to place a higher premium on your reputation than on your desire to prosper. He instructs you to choose a good name above riches.

The Bible-made millionaires of old were also men of godly character. They were men of integrity who consistently conducted their affairs in a godly and honest way. Time and time again, they chose reputation above fame. It was more important to them to be in God's *good book* than to have a *fat checkbook!*

Millionaire Joseph chose to go to prison rather than commit adultery with Potiphar's wife. Millionaire Daniel chose to eat vegetables rather than defile himself with the king's meat. God told Millionaire Abraham, *"Walk before Me and be blameless … and [I] will multiply you exceedingly"* (Genesis 17:1-2). Abraham's integrity was crucial to his being blessed of the Lord.

Likewise, if you want God to make you into a Bible-made millionaire, you must walk before Him and be upright. You must be a person of integrity. God only upholds or backs a person of integrity. If you engage in crooked practices, God cannot back you or make you rich.

> As for me, You uphold me in my integrity, And set me before Your face forever. Blessed be the LORD God of Israel From everlasting to everlasting! Amen and Amen.
>
> Psalm 41:12-13

To receive and retain the riches that God has ordained for you, you must be a person of strong Christian character. You must choose to be a person of integrity. People of strong character retain riches (see Proverbs 11:16, KJV). People of loose character will lose it (Proverbs 13:11)!

HOW TO DEVELOP INTEGRITY

Integrity is not a virtue that comes naturally. It must be deliberately cultivated, or developed through habit. Every kind of behavior, good or bad, is the product of habit. A habit is an acquired pattern of behavior that has been established through repetition. It is an act that you do so frequently that it becomes an integral part of your personality. Habits can produce good or bad behavior. Good habits produce good character. Bad habits result in bad behavior. It is as simple as that.

Ultimately, your habits will determine your quality of life, as well as your financial future. When you consistently make better choices, you create better habits. These better habits produce better character. When you have better character, you add more value to the world. When you become more valuable, you attract bigger and better opportunities. This is why integrity is so important to the Bible-made millionaire.

Prosperous people have successful habits, while non-prosperous people don't. If you desire to be a person of integrity who conducts all his works and affairs in truth, there are certain bad practices that you must drop.

There are also some good habits that you must adopt. As you embrace them, integrity will become a fundamental part of your being. It will be virtually impossible for you to compromise God's stand for anything. Here are some useful habits that will help you build and maintain a good reputation.

1. MAKE A HABIT OF TELLING THE TRUTH.

> Do not lie to one another, since you have put off the old man with his deeds, and have put on the new man who is renewed in knowledge according to the image of Him who created him.
>
> Colossians 3:9-10

You would be shocked to know that there are some believers who still tell lies, especially "business" lies. Keep in mind that in this scripture, the Apostle Paul was not writing to the unsaved. This letter was addressed to the Christians in the Colossian church!

I mentioned earlier that integrity is missing in our society to the point that corruption is not only rampant, but it also seems acceptable. It is not uncommon for Christians to join their unbelieving counterparts to try to "beat the system" by lying to make headway in business and life. They lie to evade taxes, they lie to secure contracts, they lie to obtain loans, and so forth.

Others exaggerate their services to run down the competition or to make their résumé look more attractive to prospective employers. You need to know that when you exaggerate or alter the truth it is the same thing as telling a lie. This is not the way of the Bible-made millionaire. You must hate every form of falsehood with a passion. Jesus said, *"But let your 'Yes' be 'Yes,' and your 'No,' 'No.' For whatever is more than these is from the evil one"* (Matthew 5:37).

Do not condone any kind of lie. No matter the situation, always speak the truth. Do not alter it in any way or under any circumstance. Take responsibility for your actions whenever you are wrong. Do not give excuses for your mistakes. When you are known for truth, people will trust you as a person of integrity. They will always be able to count on your word.

2. Do Not Overpromise And Underperform.

Nothing works against a reputation of integrity more than broken promises. If you are quick to make big promises, yet you fail to deliver to your employer, employees, clientele, business partners, and so forth, soon they will stop taking you seriously. They will conclude that you never mean what you say, and as such, your word or agreements cannot be counted upon. You will be considered as a person who cannot perform. As such, they will be reluctant to trust you with jobs, contracts, or assignments that could have brought you great wealth. They will choose to give these things to others who are more dependable than you.

Do not feel compelled to make exaggerated claims about your skills. If you know you can do a job, just do it! You do not need to promise heaven and earth trying to convince others of your capabilities. Instead, let your works speak for you. *Actions speak louder than words!* Jesus' works spoke louder than His words. Once in response to His skeptics, He said, "*If I do not do the works of My Father, do not believe Me; but if I do, though you do not believe Me, believe the works...*" (John 10:37-38a).

In short, Jesus was saying, "*If My words do not line up with My works, do not believe Me ... do not be convinced about My claims.*" By this, Jesus established that the power to convince others lies more in a person's works than in his words. He did not boast or brag to prove His competence; He just pointed people to His works. In the same manner, seek to convince others about your skills through your works more than your words. This way, you will avoid the temptation to make hasty promises.

You may ask, "*Well, I have never had a chance to prove my competence, so how do I sell myself?*" In this case, simply tell your prospective employer or client about whatever experience you might have had. It may not be anywhere near the magnitude of what they are asking you to do, but let them know that based on your past performances, you are willing to give their job your best shot.

This was the approach Millionaire David took when applying to King Saul for the job of killing Goliath, the great enemy of Israel. He simply told the king that he would tackle Goliath with the same winning method that he had used against his opponents in times past. He did not go overboard with his claims.

> And Saul said to David, "You are not able to go against this Philistine to fight with him; for you are a youth, and he a man of war from his youth."

> But David said to Saul, "Your servant used to keep his father's sheep, and when a lion or a bear came and took a lamb out of the flock, I went out after it and struck it, and delivered the lamb from its mouth; and when it arose against me, I caught it by its beard, and struck and killed it. Your servant has killed both lion and bear; and this uncircumcised Philistine will be like one of them, seeing he has defied the armies of the living God." Moreover David said, "The LORD, who delivered me from the paw of the lion and from the paw of the bear, He will deliver me from the hand of this Philistine." And Saul said to David, "Go, and the LORD be with you!"
>
> 1 Samuel 17:33-37

Compared to the lion and bear, Goliath seemed to be a far greater challenge. But David was able to win the king over by his willingness to do the job. David got the job that ultimately launched him into prominence without exaggeration or lies.

God will always back you when you are committed to the truth. Follow Millionaire David's example. Do not feel compelled to convince prospective employers or clients by exaggerations. Even if in your own estimation, you feel that the task is easy, keep the full details of your assessment to yourself. Do not speak all that is in your heart. Proverbs 29:11 says, *A fool uttereth all his mind: but a wise man keepeth it in till afterwards* (KJV).

It is wiser not to reveal all your plans. Save it until after you have done a great job. Even if you feel that you can exceed their expectations, do not let them know it. Then when you perform higher than they had hoped, you will build a good reputation, and they will trust you with bigger, more profitable jobs.

However, when you make balloon promises but perform lower than expected, you will lose the respect of prospective employers or clients. *You gain more respect by exceeding people's expectations instead of disappointing them.* It is better to surprise people or corporations with outstanding results than it is to let them down. In short, *it is safer to underpromise and then overperform!*

Moreover, whenever you are approached to do a job or carry out an assignment, do not feel obligated to respond immediately. Simply tell your employer or client that you need time to research about how best to tackle the challenge.

This was what Millionaire Daniel did when confronted with the assignment of interpreting King Nebuchadnezzar's dream. He was not hasty to promise the king an immediate interpretation. Instead, Daniel *went in and asked the king to give him time, that he might tell the king the interpretation (Daniel 2:16)*

Subsequently, he sought God in prayer, was given the interpretation of the king's dream, and was ultimately promoted to great honor and wealth by the king.

> Then the king promoted Daniel and gave him many great gifts; and he made him ruler over the whole province of Babylon, and chief administrator over all the wise men of Babylon.
>
> Daniel 2:48

Like Millionaire Daniel, take a good look at any task or job presented to you. Do not make any promises until you have done a thorough assessment and counted the cost. Jesus said, *"For which of you, intending to build a tower, does not sit down first and count the cost, whether he has enough to finish it"* (Luke 14:28).

Do not be hasty to reveal all that you can do. Let your works speak louder than your words. Remember, it is foolish to hastily make promises, only to break them. But when you do what you say as promised, people will respect you as a person of integrity.

3. Do Not Make Alliances With Corrupt People.

> Do not be deceived: "Evil company corrupts good habits."
>
> 1 Corinthians 15:33

You may be a person of great integrity, honest and straightforward in all your dealings. Yet if you make alliances or maintain close friendships with dishonest, corrupt, immoral, or crooked people, the Bible states clearly that their evil ways will corrupt your good habits. Remember, you need good habits to form good behavior. It is your good habits that will develop you into a person of integrity. But hanging out with the wrong crowd will sabotage all your efforts.

If, after taking so much time to form and adopt new habits, you begin to relate closely with people who lie all the way up the corporate ladder, evade taxes, tell business lies, falsify documents, and practice all manner of dishonesty, the Bible says that all your good efforts will go to waste. The bad habits of the evil company you stay with will surely corrupt your good ways.

God warned Millionaire Solomon, the wealthiest king in the Bible, not to make alliances with evil company. He told him not to marry women from any nation that did not have a covenant with the living God. Solomon was not to make any friendship with idolatrous people who neither loved God nor walked in His ways. Sadly, Solomon must have deceived himself into thinking that he could never be corrupted by evil company. He probably believed that he loved God too much and that no one was powerful or influential enough to turn him away from God. But he was wrong.

In the beginning of his days as king, Solomon loved God dearly and walked in His ways (see 1 Kings 3:3). In short, Solomon was a man of integrity. Yet, toward the end of his reign, things were no longer the same because, contrary to God's command, he had chosen to marry from the places that God had clearly forbidden. The evil company that he kept soon corrupted his good habits to the point that he no longer loved God like he once did. Eventually, Solomon fell so low that he even began to practice idolatry with his strange wives. He actually began to follow after other gods, building altars in their honor!

> But King Solomon loved many foreign women, as well as the daughter of Pharaoh: women of the Moabites, Ammonites, Edomites, Sidonians,

and Hittites—from the nations of whom the LORD had said to the children of Israel, "You shall not intermarry with them, nor they with you. Surely they will turn away your hearts after their gods." Solomon clung to these in love. And he had seven hundred wives, princesses, and three hundred concubines; and his wives turned away his heart. **For it was so, when Solomon was old, that his wives turned his heart after other gods; and his heart was not loyal to the LORD his God, as was the heart of his father David.** For Solomon went after Ashtoreth the goddess of the Sidonians, and after Milcom the abomination of the Ammonites. Solomon did evil in the sight of the LORD, and did not fully follow the LORD, as did his father David. Then Solomon built a high place for Chemosh the abomination of Moab, on the hill that is east of Jerusalem, and for Molech the abomination of the people of Ammon. And he did likewise for all his foreign wives, who burned incense and sacrificed to their gods. So the LORD became angry with Solomon, because his heart had turned from the LORD God of Israel, who had appeared to him twice, and had commanded him concerning this thing, that he should not go after other gods; but he did not keep what the LORD had commanded. **Therefore the LORD said to Solomon, "Because you have done this, and have not kept My covenant and My statutes, which I have commanded you, I will surely tear the kingdom away from you and give it to your servant."**

1 Kings 11:1-11, emphasis mine

To feel that you have such strong character that you cannot be corrupted by the bad behavior of others is to deceive yourself. The Bible says emphatically, *Do not be deceived: "Evil company corrupts good habits."* Are you wiser than God? Do you know human nature like He does? He knows the heart of man, and if He says that evil company will infect your good habits, then you better believe that it will!

You are working so hard to build a reputation of integrity. Do not ruin your efforts by forging business partnerships or close friendships with those who lack integrity. Stay away from dishonest people, and you will remain a person of integrity!

4. Constantly Evaluate Your Character.

> For if we would judge ourselves, we would not be judged. But when we are judged, we are chastened by the Lord, that we may not be condemned with the world.
>
> 1 Corinthians 11:31-32

One of the greatest assets to character development is *self- evaluation*, or what the Bible calls *self-judgment*. The word *judge* here is not a condemning word. Rather, it is a *correctioning* word. It means to search or make an honest assessment of your personality with the intention of exposing and renouncing any practice that is contrary to God's will and ways. Millionaire David, a man after God's heart, once prayed, *Search me, O God, and know my heart; try me, and know my anxieties; and see if there is any wicked way in me, and lead me in the way everlasting* (Psalm 139:23-24).

When you judge yourself, you open yourself up for God to search and expose every evil way that may be hibernating within you. You allow God to chastise you and ultimately change you by the power of His Holy Spirit.

Please understand that after all is said and done, you can only develop integrity by the power of God. Without the transforming power of God's Holy Spirit at work in your life, every effort to build a reputation of integrity will be in vain. Psalm 127:1a says, *Unless the LORD builds the house, they labor in vain who build it.*

You need His help to help develop integrity, and He will only help you when you open yourself honestly to Him. When you evaluate yourself, you allow God to chastise, or correct, every wrong in your life. God cannot work in your life and change you unless you are willing to open yourself up to Him on a continual basis for honest assessment.

From time to time, honestly go to God in prayer and pray as David did, that God would search and try you, exposing every wicked way. He will spotlight aspects of your personality that need change. He will show you an honest picture of yourself. He does not do this to condemn you. He does it to correct you. He wants to remove any evil tendency in your heart and establish His good way in you.

He may reveal to you that you are too hasty in your speech. He might warn you about a friendship you are involved in or a partnership that you are considering. He may reprove you about your failure to stick to deadlines or keep appointments. Whatever it is that God points out to you, do not resist His chastening. When God shows you a wrong, admit it. Do not spare yourself. Do not point fingers. Remember, you are in the presence of the One who sees and knows all.

Not only will He expose any bad habit in your life, but He will also show you how to adopt new ones. He will lead you in the way everlasting. Embrace His correction in a spirit of humility, and God will give you the grace to drop that bad practice.

Those who do not evaluate their character on a constant basis leave no room for God to work in their lives. If you want Him to make you into a person of integrity, you must constantly yield yourself to Him through self-judgment.

You may also ask the honest opinion of those who love you and whom you respect, people who will not massage your ego. They should be people who are not afraid to confront you with your wrong. *They should speak the truth to you in love—they should tell you what you need to hear, not what you want to hear!* Make yourself fully accountable to those whom God has put in authority over you and determine that you will take their correction seriously.

Most people who lack integrity do so because they lack accountability. It is hard for you not to develop integrity when you are fully accountable to those whom God has made responsible for you. Those who make themselves accountable understand that they cannot just do what they feel like doing because there is someone who will hold them responsible for their actions.

If you desire to develop integrity, you must never be afraid of facing up to an honest assessment of yourself. Consult the people whom you love and respect. Let them help you *nip in the bud*, every bad habit in your life before they become your established behavioral patterns.

Come before the Lord. Ask Him to search all your endeavors. Ask Him to reveal to you anything that displeases Him in the way you conduct your business or your work. Pray to Him from the depths of your heart, saying, *[Lord], let integrity and uprightness preserve me, for I wait for You* (Psalm 25:21).

WHERE INTEGRITY IS DISREGARDED, DESTINY IS DOOMED!

There is a consequence for every action and lifestyle. A person who chooses to disregard integrity in his quest for wealth and success is setting himself up for future disaster. Though he may attain wealth, and even become a millionaire, ultimately his nemesis will catch up with him. His flawed character will be his undoing.

There are several examples of people who once were wealthy, but because of their corrupt lifestyles, lost everything faster than they had gained it. There is no question about it: Where integrity is disregarded, destiny is doomed!

If you desire to secure a strong financial future for yourself and your children, you must pay close attention to the matter of integrity. Without a doubt, integrity is one of the most important secrets of Bible-made millionaires.

Not only will integrity help you attain wealth, but it will also help you sustain it. When you walk in integrity, God will fight every opposition to your success. You will never slip away from the position of honor and wealth that God has given you. Integrity will establish you in success. It will vindicate you and establish you in perpetual wealth.

> Vindicate me, O LORD, For I have walked in my integrity. I have also trusted in the LORD; I shall not slip. Examine me, O LORD, and prove me; Try my mind and my heart. For Your lovingkindness is before my eyes, And I have walked in Your truth. I have not sat with idolatrous mortals, Nor will I go in with hypocrites. I have hated the assembly of evildoers, And will not sit with the wicked.
>
> Psalm 26:1-4

Integrity is a securer of financial destiny! When you walk in integrity, you will never be demoted from your millionaire status. You will not prosper today, only to become a pauper tomorrow. No! Therefore, do not strive to make money. Take the time to develop integrity based on the principles that I have shared. Strive to maintain your integrity.

When I was leaving the denomination that I had served for a decade, God told me not to take a single thing from the ministry—not even the possessions to which I was entitled. I remember someone had bought me the beautiful desk that I used in my office. Though he had specifically stated that the desk was a personal gift to me and not the church, God said I was not to take it. He said that if I did, I would sabotage my destiny.

I knew my future was too bright to be traded for a mere morsel of bread, so I obeyed God. I did not take a dime from that place. I chose to walk in integrity. As a result, I have seen God prevail for me time and time again. He establishes my goings so that my feet never slip. Integrity is one of the most priceless things to me, and I trust Him to help me walk in integrity all the days of my life.

Friend, if you want to change your financial status, change your ways. If you keep on doing what you have always done, you will keep on having the results that you have always gotten. Clearly identify your bad or unproductive habits and drop them. Adopt new integrity-producing habits, and you will secure for yourself an enduring place in the millionaire club.

Chapter 7

Secret #5: Be Persistent in Faith

> A faithful man will abound with blessings, But he who hastens to be rich will not go unpunished.
>
> Proverbs 28:20

So far, we have discovered that becoming wealthy the Bible way requires a strong devotion to God, a God-given purpose, well-mapped-out strategies, and the quality of integrity. Another very vital element in the journey to godly riches is persistence. If you desire to become a Bible-made millionaire, you must always maintain unflinching faith in God's promise to prosper you.

Many have started their journey to wealth with so much enthusiasm, only to give up along the way when confronted with tough situations. When they first heard of God's plan to prosper them, they were excited and had honestly expected to become millionaires overnight. But when the riches that they desired seemed slow in coming, they gave up hope and accepted mediocre or low level living as their lot in life. They concluded that they were probably not destined to be millionaires. As a result, they chose to settle for the status quo.

Friend, you must not fall into this error. Remember, *your wealth is not a matter of chance. It is matter of covenant.* Wealth is the believer's portion by *right*, not by *random selection! All those who are of faith* are entitled to Abraham's blessings, including his great riches. No Christian is left out.

Do not ever forget that as a covenant child of God, wealth is your due. It is your inheritance. You *can* and *should* be wealthy. However, you need to understand that godly prosperity is not gained *overnight*. It is attained *over time*.

The Bible clearly states that becoming rich in a quick and hasty way is definitely not the way to wealth. Wealth gained hurriedly will disappear almost just as fast. Records confirm that a number of those who become instant millionaires through the lottery become broke only a few years after. There was a case of a woman who won $4 million in the Virginia lottery. Barely a decade later, not only had she lost all of her winnings, she also had incurred a debt of over $150,000! This confirms the wisdom of Scripture, which says:

> The plans of the diligent lead surely to plenty, But those of everyone who is **hasty**, surely to poverty.
>
> Proverbs 21:5, emphasis mine

> A man with an evil eye hastens after riches, And does not consider that poverty will come upon him.
>
> Proverbs 28:22

Anyone who desires to become rich God's way must be willing to invest time, effort, and a good deal of patience. Bible-made millionaires realize this, and that is why no matter what confronts them in their journey to success, they never quit. Though things may get tough, they keep going. They do not stop. They continue to forge ahead amidst the most trying of circumstances.

In your journey to prosperity and millionaire status, there will be hurdles and obstacles that you will face. This is inevitable. Jesus said that in the world you will have tribulation (John 16:33). Yet if you want to enjoy the *pleasure* of godly prosperity, you must be willing to confront the *pressures* of the world head-on. Never run away, because *you cannot conquer what you are not willing to confront.* Quitters never win, and winners never quit!

There is no crown without a cross. You cannot be pronounced a winner if you have never fought and won a battle. So determine to resist every enemy of your prosperity. Remain strong in faith, and you will emerge a perpetual winner in the race of life.

No devil in hell or tribulation of this world can defeat the indomitable force of faith. In the battles of life, faith always delivers victory. Faith triumphs and prevails over the obstacles that try to hinder a person in his quest for success. Faith will always, without fail, move your mountains!

> So Jesus answered and said to them, "Have faith in God. For assuredly, I say to you, whoever says to this mountain, 'Be removed and be cast into the sea,' and does not doubt in his heart, but believes that those things he says will be done, he will have whatever he says."
>
> Mark 11:22-23

No matter the tribulation or trial, if you have unwavering faith in God, you will emerge a winner over that situation. You will overcome! First John 5:4 says, *For whatever is born of God overcomes the world. And this is the **victory** that has overcome the world—our faith* (emphasis mine).

Hurdles That You Must Overcome

In your journey to success and prosperity, the obstacles that confront you will come in the form of either 1) critical voices, or 2) contrary circumstances. Sometimes it is possible for a person to face both hurdles at the same time.

1. Critical Voices

There are two types of criticism: negative criticism and constructive criticism.

> Do not correct a scoffer, lest he hate you; Rebuke a wise man, and he will love you. Give instruction to a wise man, and he will be still wiser; Teach a just man, and he will increase in learning.
>
> Proverbs 9:8-9

As the name implies, constructive criticism is good and targets positive results. It is the honest evaluation of a person, thing, or enterprise for the purpose of improvement and progress. It is pursued by champions the world over. Wise and financially successful people appreciate the value of positive criticism. They understand that when taken and adhered to, such criticism has the power to make them more effective, skillful, and productive in their endeavors.

> Strike a scoffer, and the simple will become wary;
> Rebuke one who has understanding, and he will discern knowledge.
>
> Proverbs 19:25

As a prospective Bible-made millionaire, you must always be in a position where you are willing to be open to positive and productive scrutiny. You must be open to the viewpoints or analyses of others. This will expand your scope of vision and help accelerate your progress.

On the other hand, negative criticism is destructive and demeaning. Its effects are adverse. It is not advantageous. It is someone's antagonistic, subjective viewpoint of another person, thing, or enterprise.

In your quest to become a Bible-made millionaire, you must be able to tell the difference between constructive and negative criticism. Embrace positive criticism, but reject negative criticism. Here are some tips that can help you distinguish between the two:

CONSTRUCTIVE CRITICISM:

- ✓ Is honest and objective in its outlook. Positive criticism seeks to affirm and encourage.
- ✓ Points to your potential. It targets improvement.
- ✓ Is borne out of genuine love.
- ✓ Inspires and motivates.

NEGATIVE CRITICISM:

- ✓ Is subjective. It is antagonistic and demeaning.
- ✓ Is finger-pointing and fault-finding in nature. It verbally attacks your person and your purpose. Its aim is to destroy, not improve. It seeks to demolish morale, and ultimately, dreams.
- ✓ Flows out of hate, envy, and jealousy. It also has the capacity of ruining relationships.
- ✓ Generates destructive emotions that affect a person's emotional, physical, and social well-being. This, in turn, affects a person's ability to perform.

While you should embrace positive criticism, you must diligently guard against negative criticism. Do not ever let it affect you or cause you to give up your desire to prosper or advance in life.

Millionaire Joseph was the subject of negative criticism from his jealous brothers. Out of jealousy they criticized their brother and attacked his dreams with harsh, hateful words.

> Now Joseph had a dream, and he told it to his brothers; and they hated him even more. So he said to them, "Please hear this dream which I have dreamed: There we were, binding sheaves in the field. Then behold, my sheaf arose and

> also stood upright; and indeed your sheaves stood all around and bowed down to my sheaf." And his brothers said to him, "Shall you indeed reign over us? Or shall you indeed have dominion over us?" So they hated him even more for his dreams and for his words.
>
> Genesis 37:5-8

Yet Joseph did not allow his brothers' negative words to get to him. Even after his brothers sold him into slavery, he maintained the image of greatness that God had revealed to him about himself, and he portrayed himself accordingly. As such, even in captivity, he did not look like a downtrodden slave. He looked regal and dignified, *handsome in form and appearance* (Genesis 39:6). Millionaire Joseph went on to fulfill his dreams in spite of his brothers' antagonisms, because he did not allow himself to be limited by their negative words. Instead, he chose to remain motivated by God's Word.

Unless you know how to handle negative criticism, it can affect your self-image and esteem. It can change how you view yourself and your capabilities. It can make you think less of yourself than you really are. In this sense, it paralyzes initiative, which is greatly needed for success. It kills creativity and enthusiasm. A person who has allowed negative criticism to affect him will lack the motivation required to pursue his vision or dream. Such a person will no longer act on his purpose, for fear of looking stupid or foolish before his critics.

There are those who will tell you very convincingly a thousand and one reasons why you cannot become wealthy. They will laugh at your dreams and mock your aspirations.

Some people may even label you as proud and ambitious. This was what Millionaire David's brothers called him after he had openly declared his intention to destroy Goliath, the great enemy of Israel.

> Then David spoke to the men who stood by him, saying, "What shall be done for the man who kills this Philistine and takes away the reproach from Israel? For who is this uncircumcised Philistine, that he should defy the armies of the living God?" And the people answered him in this manner, saying, "So shall it be done for the man who kills him." Now Eliab his oldest brother heard when he spoke to the men; and Eliab's anger was aroused against David, and he said, "Why did you come down here? And with whom have you left those few sheep in the wilderness? I know your pride and the insolence of your heart, for you have come down to see the battle." And David said, "What have I done now? Is there not a cause?" Then he turned from him toward another and said the same thing; and these people answered him as the first ones did.
>
> 1 Samuel 17:26-30

Though Eliab's criticism was harsh and sharp, David did not pay attention to him. Instead, he affirmed his dream in the presence of his critic. He said boldly to Eliab, "*Is there not a cause?*" And he did something else—*he turned from him toward another.* Not only did David stick to his vision, he also shifted his position away from his negative critic. This is how you should handle your negative critics. Affirm your vision in their presence, and then move away from them. Do not remain in the presence of negativity. If you want to be blessed and prosperous in all that you do, you must not keep company with scornful, fault-finding, critical people (see Psalm 1:1-3).

In Mark 5, the principle that you can only progress and make headway in life by separating yourself from negative critics is affirmed by our Lord. Before He could raise Jairus's daughter from the dead, the Lord first put out the negative critics. He separated Himself from all those who ridiculed His mission and laughed Him to scorn.

Likewise, to become the Bible-made millionaire that God has ordained you to be, you must move away from antagonistic, negative people. It doesn't matter how long you have known them. If anyone has a negative effect on you or your mission, you must move away from them. Association is not by force. It is by choice!

You cannot please everyone. So do not dignify negative critics with a response. Do not try to plead with them to see your point of view. Understand that in the pursuit of your life's mission, you owe no man an explanation for your God-given purpose. You only owe God your obedience! Jesus never responded to negative critics. He always focused on doing the will of His Father.

Unfortunately, some people bow under the pressure of negative criticism. They throw away their dreams because of the harsh words of jealous, narrow-minded people. Trying to please everyone is a sure way to fail. Being controlled by the opinions of others is the surest way of missing God's purpose for your life. For those who choose to pursue the plans of other people, failure is the most likely outcome.

Friend, please do not let your dreams perish at the hands of negative voices. You are not what other people say you are—*you are who God says you are!*

God gave you the power to get wealth, so who on earth can refute it? God gave you a dream, who is he that can render it impossible? Believe God alone. Hold on to His word for you, and face your assignment. Like David and our Lord Jesus, turn away from negative critics and give yourself fully to your God-given dream.

Boldly declare in the words of Isaiah 50: *For the Lord GOD will help Me; therefore I will not be disgraced; therefore I have set My face like a flint, and I know that I will not be ashamed. He is near who justifies Me; who will contend with Me? Let us stand together. Who is My adversary? Let him come near Me. Surely the Lord GOD will help Me; who is he who will condemn Me? Indeed they will all grow old like a garment; The moth will eat them up* (verses 7-9).

Your negative critics will grow old like a garment. They will not be permitted to rave against you forever, because the moth will eat them up. They fade away, but your God-given promise will stay.

Bible-made millionaires prosper and become rich because they know how to deal with negative criticism. Do not let the voices of negative critics dictate the pace of your progress in life. Do not pay attention to strange, contrary voices. Listen to God's voice alone.

2. Contrary Circumstances

The word *contrary* means to be opposite in nature, in purpose or in direction. A contrary circumstance is an experience that is drastically different from what was expected.

In your journey to abundant wealth, it will not be uncommon for you to encounter unexpected situations that are in direct opposition to the prosperity that God has promised you. It could be an unexpected layoff, an aggressive competitor that is threatening to take away your market base, a large employee turnover, a prospective business deal that failed to materialize, and so forth.

These contrary situations are orchestrated by the enemy to dispute and hinder God's promise in your life. Through them, satan will try to steal, kill, and destroy every dream that God has birthed in your heart. Jesus said that tribulation or persecution would arise on account of the Word, which is the promise that you received from God.

> "But he who received the seed on stony places, this is he who hears the word and immediately receives it with joy; yet he has no root in himself, but endures only for a while. For when tribulation or persecution arises because of the word, immediately he stumbles."
>
> Mark 13:20-21

God has promised that wealth is your portion in Christ. But the devil, through persecution and tribulation, will try to counteract God's good purpose. Even after he was anointed king, Millionaire David went through tough times before he eventually ascended to the throne.

God gave Millionaire Joseph dreams of wealth and greatness while he was yet a teenager. But before those dreams became reality, he encountered the pit, slavery, and prison.

No sooner than Millionaire Abraham began his journey to prosperity, he encountered a great famine. A few years after, Millionaire Isaac had a similar experience.

Millionaire Daniel had to pass through the lion's den before he was promoted to a higher level of power and affluence.

Millionaire Jacob faced hardship and injustice at the hand of his uncle, Laban, before he became a wealthy rancher.

Shortly after our Lord Jesus was affirmed as the Son of God at His spectacular water baptism, He was thrust into the barren wilderness to be tempted by the devil.

Friend, know for sure that in your journey to riches, you will encounter tough situations or seasons. This is inevitable. Testimony after testimony in Scripture proves the point that contrary circumstances will come. But if properly handled, trials can actually pave the way to the greatness that God has promised you. Trials can be stepping- stones to your success. After the Lord overcame the trials that He faced in the wilderness, He returned in the power of the Holy Spirit and immediately His fame went forth (see Luke 4:14).

Possession is only for those who are willing to contend against the enemy. God promised to bring the children of Israel into a wealthy place, into a land flowing with milk and honey. Yet before they could possess the land, they had to fight and conquer the enemies that stood in their way.

> "Rise, take your journey, and cross over the River Arnon. Look, I have given into your hand Sihon the Amorite, king of Heshbon, and his land. Begin to possess it, and engage him in battle."
>
> Deuteronomy 2:24

Beloved, though trials of life are inevitable, you need to know that if you choose to fight and not give up, your victory is sure. As tough as contrary circumstances may seem, do not let them stop you. Do not succumb to the pressures of opposition, because God has empowered you to triumph victoriously over them. In Christ, you have the power to triumph always and in all things.

> Now thanks be to God who always leads us in triumph in Christ.
>
> 2 Corinthians 2:14a

Bible-made millionaires of old did not give up their vision in the face of desperate circumstances. Rather, they persisted, and ultimately they came out victorious. When Millionaire Isaac encountered famine, his first instinct was to run away. He did not want to face it. But God told him to stay and face up to the challenge. He obeyed, and as a result, God prospered him there. He gained mastery over the famine and prospered exceedingly in the direst of circumstances.

> There was a famine in the land, besides the first famine that was in the days of Abraham. And Isaac went to Abimelech king of the Philistines, in Gerar. Then the LORD appeared to him and said: "Do not go down to Egypt; live in the land of which I shall tell you. Dwell in this land, and I

> will be with you and bless you; for to you and your descendants I give all these lands, and I will perform the oath which I swore to Abraham your father."
> Then Isaac sowed in that land, and reaped in the same year a hundredfold; and the LORD blessed him. The man began to prosper, and continued prospering until he became very prosperous; for he had possessions of flocks and possessions of herds and a great number of servants. So the Philistines envied him.
>
> Genesis 26:1-3, 12-14

Likewise, to be a Bible-made millionaire, you must choose never to run away from or give in to tough situations. Face them head-on! When you face life's battles full of faith, you will win. But those who run away cannot receive the trophies of war. Tough times are temporary, but the promise of God to prosper you is enduring.

How to Stay Persistent in Faith

> Looking unto Jesus, the author and finisher of our faith, who for the joy that was set before Him endured the cross, despising the shame, and has sat down at the right hand of the throne of God.
>
> Hebrews 12:2

The two simple and practical keys for maintaining persistent faith are encoded in this verse. They are:

1. Your ability to stay focused on Jesus.
2. Your ability to stay focused on your goal and the reward that it brings.

It is absolutely impossible for your faith to fail when your eyes are fixed on Jesus and set on the joyful reward of your God-given promise. If you desire to ascend the throne of glory and wealth that God has prepared for you, you must embrace these principles with all your heart.

1. Stay Focused on Jesus.

First, you must stay focused on Jesus.

What does this mean? It means that you make a conscious effort, in the midst of life's storms, to concentrate on God's *power* and not the *problem*; on His *ability* and not the *adversity*.

It means that at all times you must remember that God is your Present Help in time of need. You know that His power to save you is far greater than the enemy's ability to persecute you. So you preoccupy your thoughts with His infallible, unchanging Word because you know that no matter how fiery the trial, God has already prepared an escape route for you (see 1 Corinthians 10:13). It is impossible for you to be trapped or stranded in life.

More specifically, where your prosperity is concerned, never forget that the promise for your wealth did not originate from you; it came from God. It was He who said, "*I have given you the power to get wealth.*" It was He who birthed in your heart the desire to prosper. You understand that He is able to finish what He authored.

Isaiah 66:9 tells us: "*Shall I bring to the time of birth, and not cause delivery?" says the LORD. "Shall I who cause delivery shut up the womb?" says your God.* God is capable of delivering every dream that He caused you to conceive. He is well able to complete what He started. So choose not to be moved by anything that happens in between. If God said you will prosper, then you will prosper, no matter what!

Though the temptation to quit may be strong, remain persistent in faith, and you will prevail. Maintain faith in God who gave you the power to get wealth, and maintain faith in the possibility of your God-given dream. You know from Scripture that wealth is your portion. Remain confident in the fact that no force of hell, no trial or circumstance of life, can hinder God from fulfilling His promise in your life. No one can reverse His blessings that were meant for you.

> "Indeed before the day was, I am He; And there is no one who can deliver out of My hand; I work, and who will reverse it?"
>
> Isaiah 43:13

A good way to keep your focus on the Lord is through worship and praise. Give glory to God in all things. Rejoice evermore! This was something Millionaire David did often when he faced tough times. During a very trying time in his life while he was fleeing King's Saul's jealous wrath, he sang, *"I will bless the LORD at all times; His praise shall continually be in my mouth"* (Psalm 34:1).

Someone said that if the devil cannot steal your joy, he cannot take your goods. The devil cannot deprive you of your rich heritage as long as you choose to rejoice in God always. When you magnify God through praise and worship, you will discover that you will think less of the problem and more of His power. God's praise will drown the voice of every critic and make a mockery out of every bad report.

2. STAY FOCUSED ON YOUR GOAL AND THE REWARD THAT IT BRINGS.

Second, to maintain persistent faith, you must stay focused on your goal. Never lose sight of your God-given vision and the rich reward that it will bring. Jesus endured—refused to give up in the face of trial—*because of the joy that was set before Him*. You need to always keep a clear vision of your reward in your mind. This will inspire you and motivate you to move on in the toughest of situations. When you remember what is at stake and what there is to gain, you will not give up your dream for anything.

Now notice that the verse says that joy was set *before* Him. It was not behind Him. In other words, Jesus looked forward; He never looked back. Friend, to maintain your faith, you must never look back. There is nothing to look forward to in your past! Do not look at past failures or disappointments. These will dampen and kill your faith. Never look behind; always look before you ... your future is bright!

To be forward-looking is to be an optimist. An optimist is a forward- thinking person who always believes that no matter the situation, the best will always happen to him. An optimist always has a positive outlook to life's situations and circumstances. Optimists are usually the happiest, healthiest, most successful, and most influential people on earth.

Most of the time, optimists think about what they want and how to get it. They do not preoccupy themselves with the obstacles or problems that they encounter along the way. They look for solutions. They do not magnify problems. They think more about where they are going and how to get there. As a result, they have the ability to prosper in the most adverse of situations.

During the Great Depression of the early twentieth century, while many companies folded, the Chrysler Corporation, a famous American automobile company, prospered and flourished. The success of Chrysler amid the longest and most severe economic depression ever experienced by the industrialized Western world had a lot to do with the optimism and foresight of its founder, Walter Percy Chrysler. Though he had every reason to experience anxiety about the Great Depression, he chose not to. While others saw dark times, he saw a bright future. Undeterred by the adverse economic climate that engulfed the world, Mr. Chrysler ventured into an area where others, because of the dismal times, had steered away from. This was the area of research and development, an aspect for which his company later became famous.

Beloved, are you going through tough times? Be encouraged—the future is bright! Behind every cloud is a silver lining. No matter how dark your night, it will surely give way to the morning! Do not fill your mind with the images of despair. No! Keep your God-given dream always before your eyes.

The very idea of thinking about your glorious future is a tremendous faith booster. As long as you know that you have something to look forward to, you will keep going. You will be full of energy and creativity. This, in turn, will motivate and stimulate you to perform at peak levels, regardless of the circumstances.

You become what you think about most of the time. How you think about any situation will determine how you feel, and your feelings will determine your behavior. If you want to maintain faith, you must be a lifelong optimist. Think good and godly thoughts always.

> Finally, brethren, whatever things are true, whatever things are noble, whatever things are just, whatever things are pure, whatever things are lovely, whatever things are of good report, if there is any virtue and if there is anything praiseworthy—meditate on these things. The things which you learned and received and heard and saw in me, these do, and the God of peace will be with you.
>
> Philippians 4:8-9

Remember, Bible-made millionaires could persist in faith because they were extremely optimistic. They did not have a gloomy outlook on life. Their optimism propelled them to keep moving on against all odds. Millionaire Job, in the heat of his trial, confidently declared, "*But He knows the way that I take; when He has tested me, I shall come forth as gold*" (Job 23:10).

Job's optimism and unrelenting faith paid off big time! After his trying time, *Job really did come out as gold.* God literally restored back to him double for his trouble!

> And the LORD restored Job's losses when he prayed for his friends. **Indeed the LORD gave Job twice as much as he had before.**

> **Now the LORD blessed the latter days of Job more than his beginning**; for he had fourteen thousand sheep, six thousand camels, one thousand yoke of oxen, and one thousand female donkeys.
>
> Job 42:10, 12, emphasis mine

So in the midst of life's toughest situations, maintain a positive attitude. Get out of the realm of doubt and move into the realm of faith. Choose to believe God for the best even in the worst of environments.

WHEN YOU *BELIEVE*, YOU WILL *BECOME!*

Persistent faith is your ability to maintain hope in the midst of a seemingly hopeless situation. Persistent faith says, *"Since it is God's will for me to prosper, then I will surely prosper. It may not look like it now, but I will not be deceived by outward looks. I choose to believe God's promise alone. I choose not to give in to the pressures that confront me. I know that through the power of God, I will be victorious over them."*

The Bible's most prominent millionaires confronted and conquered incredible odds in their journey to wealth.

Millionaire Abraham is a great example of this. Concerning him, the Bible says in Romans 4:

> (As it is written, "I have made you a father of many nations") in the presence of Him whom he believed—God, who gives life to the dead and calls those things which do not exist as though they did; who, contrary to hope, in hope believed,

> so that he became the father of many nations, according to what was spoken, "So shall your descendants be." And not being weak in faith, he did not consider his own body, already dead (since he was about a hundred years old), and the deadness of Sarah's womb. He did not waver at the promise of God through unbelief, but was strengthened in faith, giving glory to God, and being fully convinced that what He had promised He was also able to perform (verses 17-21).

Even when it seemed as if he had no reason to be hopeful, Millionaire Abraham refused to give up hope. He stayed *"in hope." He did not fall out of hope.* He maintained firm faith in God's promise. He did not consider the many things that seemed to work against him. He gave no regard to the countless reasons *(or people)* that said his case was impossible. Instead, he chose to believe God alone. And because he persisted in faith, because he believed, he became all that God said he would be.

Friend, *when you believe, you will become!*

When you believe God's Word against all odds, you will become all that God said you will be. Faith fertilizes hope. Faith gives substance to hope and then delivers victory to you. When you believe that wealth is your portion in Christ, you will become the millionaire that God has ordained you to be. Alleluia!

Even if, peradventure, you experience defeat, understand that it is not over until God says it is over! Just because you lose one battle does not mean that you have lost the war. If you do not keep on going, you will be grounded. So you cannot afford to stop. Keep pressing forward. You have God's promise that you will rise again.

> For a righteous man may fall seven times And rise again,
> But the wicked shall fall by calamity.
>
> Proverbs 24:16

Beloved, *nothing can work against you when you maintain faith in the truth that God's Word is working for you!* Persistent faith will bring you into the wealth that God has promised you. This is why Millionaire Isaac persisted and prospered even in the midst of a great famine.

> There was a famine in the land, besides the first famine that was in the days of Abraham. And Isaac went to Abimelech king of the Philistines, in Gerar. Then the LORD appeared to him and said: "Do not go down to Egypt; live in the land of which I shall tell you. Dwell in this land, and I will be with you and bless you; for to you and your descendants I give all these lands, and I will perform the oath which I swore to Abraham your father."
> Then Isaac sowed in that land, and reaped in the same year a hundredfold; and the LORD blessed him. The man began to prosper, and continued prospering until he became very prosperous; for he had possessions of flocks and possessions of herds and a great number of servants. So the Philistines envied him.
>
> Genesis 26:1-3, 12-14

Millionaire David did not start life as a wealthy man. He began as a humble shepherd boy, the least of his father's sons. Even after the prophet Samuel anointed him as king, he did not all of a sudden begin to live a royal lifestyle. On the contrary, he lived life as a homeless fugitive running from cave to cave to escape the fury of jealous King Saul. Yet in the midst of his trials and tribulations, he maintained strong faith in God. Once, during a very trying time in his life, he sang:

> The LORD is my light and my salvation; Whom shall I fear?
> The LORD is the strength of my life; Of whom shall I be afraid? When the wicked came against me To eat up my flesh, My enemies and foes, They stumbled and fell.
> Though an army may encamp against me, My heart shall not fear; Though war may rise against me, In this I will be confident. … For in the time of trouble He shall hide me in His pavilion; In the secret place of His tabernacle He shall hide me; He shall set me high upon a rock. And now my head shall be lifted up above my enemies all around me; Therefore I will offer sacrifices of joy in His tabernacle; I will sing, yes, I will sing praises to the LORD.
>
> Psalm 27:1-3, 5-6

David knew that his tough days were only temporary, but the favor of God is forever. In another place he sang, *Weeping may endure for a night, but joy comes in the morning*. (Psalm 30:5).

He knew that *God's enduring Word will always outlast life's toughest trials*. As a result, he chose to hold on to God's promise regardless of the circumstances. Eventually David's persistent faith paid off big time! Ultimately he was enthroned as the king of all of Israel, and the wealth and splendor that God promised him became physically manifested in his life. He became one of Israel's wealthiest kings, giving personal monetary offerings of millions of dollars for the construction of God's holy temple.

Friend, regardless of what you are going through today, never doubt for one moment that your tomorrow will be better. Do not be deceived by dark trials. God's Word declares that they will not last forever. *Weeping may endure for a night, but joy comes in the morning* (Psalm 30:5).

Your account may be in a coma now. You may be up to your neck in debt. You may have been unemployed for many months. But I tell you, it is not over. God is not through with you. His favor toward you is enduring. The power of His Word will outlast the fury of your trial. Your tough days will pass away. Yes, they will! But God's good promise for your prosperity will stay. You will be the person of wealth that God has ordained you to be to the glory of His holy name!

Since the beginning of creation, even the darkest of nights have not been able to prevent the dawning of a bright new day. So I decree to you as a servant of the Most High God: Your night season is ending. You are on the verge of the dawn of a glorious new day. Put the darkness of the past behind you. Your future is bright! Tough times never last, only tough people do! Give God praise!

Chapter 8

Secret #6: Be a Wise Money Manager

> "I, wisdom, dwell with prudence, And find out knowledge and discretion. Riches and honor are with me, Enduring riches and righteousness."
>
> Proverbs 8:12, 18

Many poor people today are not broke because they do not make enough money. They are broke because they do not know how to wisely manage the money that they have.

It is one thing for you to make lots and lots of money. It is another thing for you to know how to handle it. To be a millionaire you must know what to do with money when it comes into your hand. It is your ability to be a good steward of your God-given money that will determine whether or not you will be a millionaire. Millionaire Solomon was not rich just because he made lots of money. He was rich because he was wise and prudent.

> "Blessed be the LORD God of Israel, who made heaven and earth, for He has given King David a wise son, endowed with prudence and understanding, who will build a temple for the LORD and a royal house for himself!"
>
> 2 Chronicles 2:12

The problem of poverty has more to do with a lack of wisdom than a lack of funds. There are many who can testify of making large amounts of money at some point in their lives, yet today they are on welfare or earn much lower than they once did.

> Do not say, "Why were the former days better than these?" For you do not inquire wisely concerning this. Wisdom is good with an inheritance, And profitable to those who see the sun. For wisdom is a defense as money is a defense, But the excellence of knowledge is that wisdom gives life to those who have it.
>
> Ecclesiastes 7:10-12

Many who at one time or the other could boast of a comfortable, affluent life, are repeating these words today. Sadly they ask, "*Why were the former days better than these present days?*" Many who once made millions are today drowning in debt. Others are filling for bankruptcy, having to give up prized properties and possessions that they had once cherished.

Disillusioned and perplexed, they wonder how they could fall so low after they had been so high financially. When they remember how much money they had once *owned*, they cannot fathom the amount of money they now *owe*!

But the answer to this financial dilemma is crystal-clear from this verse: *Wisdom is good with an inheritance, and profitable to those who see the sun. For wisdom is a defense as money is a defense.*

There is no question about it, wealth and riches are your inheritance in Christ. But without wisdom, that is, the wise, prudent management of your wealth, your inheritance will do you no good. Most of those who had riches in their former days lost it because they lacked wisdom. Wisdom and riches go hand in hand. Where you have wisdom, you will have riches: *Wisdom is a defense just as money is a defense.*

Friend, let this truth sink deep into your heart: *Wisdom is good with an inheritance.* In other words, without wisdom, your inheritance is not good. It is useless. Are Abraham's blessings yours? Oh, yes! Has God given you all things richly to enjoy? No question about it! Has He given you the power to get wealth? Absolutely! But God's great and wonderful provision for your wealth will not profit you if you do not know how to handle your money wisely.

On the other hand, *wisdom is good with an inheritance, and profitable.* Simply put, *wisdom plus inheritance equals profit!* When you combine wisdom with your rich inheritance, you will be properly positioned to profit from the great wealth that is yours in Christ. You will be set to become the millionaire that God ordained you to be.

The Prodigal Son: A Classic Case of Money Mismanagement

A rich inheritance will do you no good if you lack wisdom. Wisdom with inheritance is *profitable*, but inheritance without wisdom leads to *penury*. Such is the bitter lesson that the prodigal son learned.

> *Then He said: "A certain man had two sons. And the younger of them said to his father, 'Father, give me the portion of goods that falls to me.' So he divided to them his livelihood. And not many days after, the younger son* **gathered all together**, *journeyed to a far country, and there* **wasted his possessions with prodigal living.** *But when he* **had spent all**, *there arose a severe famine in that land, and he began to be in want. Then he went and joined himself to a citizen of that country, and he sent him into his fields to feed swine. And he would gladly have filled his stomach with the pods that the swine ate, and no one gave him anything."*
>
> Luke 15:11-16, emphasis mine

In Jesus' Parable of the Prodigal Son, we see how the prodigal son fell from the riches of his father's palace to the rags of the pig's pit. We see how a once wealthy man became so poor that he literally had to contend with pigs for their food rations!

The foolish way in which he handled his inheritance reveals three classic traits of a typical poor money manager. Just one or a combination of these foolish steps is enough to make a mockery of a person's financial destiny. You must avoid these errors if you want to become a Bible-made millionaire. Let us now examine the three distinct traits of poor money managers:

1. THEY ARE *GREEDY*. THEY ARE NOT GIVERS.

The Bible says that the first thing the prodigal son did after he received his inheritance was to gather it all together: *"And not many days after, the younger son* ***gathered all together"*** *(emphasis mine).* The word gather means "to collect." One of the principal reasons why people do not keep or multiply their money is because they greedily hoard or keep it to themselves.

> There is one who scatters, yet increases more; And there is one who withholds more than is right, But it leads to poverty.
>
> Proverbs 11:24

Beloved, beware of covetousness and greed. They do not lead to proserity; they lead to poverty. Moreover, they are deadly destiny destroyers. Gehazi, the servant and heir-apparent to Elisha, lost his promising destiny because of his greed (see 2 Kings 5:20-27). *Contentment brings gain, but greed brings pain!*

> Now godliness with contentment is great gain. For we brought nothing into this world, and it is certain we can carry nothing out. And having food and clothing, with these we shall be content. But those who desire to be rich fall into temptation and a snare, and into many foolish and harmful lusts which drown men in destruction and perdition. For the love of money is a root of all kinds of evil, for which some have strayed from the faith in their greediness, and pierced themselves through with many sorrows.
>
> 1 Timothy 6:6-10

God never meant for you to accumulate or keep your wealth to yourself. He wants you to distribute it for His glory. Remember the reasons for wealth that we discussed earlier on. God wants you to be giving, not greedy; a distributor, not a collector! Those who amass their God-given wealth for themselves and do not use it as God commands will end up losing it.

2. They are wasters. They are not wise spenders.

Next, the Bible says that the prodigal son "journeyed to a far country, and there **wasted his possessions with prodigal living**" (emphasis mine). Wasteful, frivolous spending is another common characteristic of a foolish money manager. To waste money means to use, consume, and spend it carelessly and without thought.

Earlier on, I mentioned that anyone who does not understand the purpose of money will ultimately abuse or misuse it. Those who handle their inheritance foolishly do so because they do not understand the God-ordained purpose for their wealth. They treat money like a toy to play around with. They fail to respect it as an important tool that God has put in their hands to accomplish His purpose.

As a result, their expenditure is driven by materialism and greed. They are not mission or kingdom-minded in their spending. It is clear from the story of the prodigal son that those who lavishly spend on pleasure will ultimately end up in poverty.

> He who loves pleasure will be a poor man; He who loves wine and oil will not be rich.
>
> Proverbs 21:17

If you desire to become the Bible-made millionaire that God ordained you to be, you must spend your money in accordance with God's purpose. Do not spend your money aimlessly or without thought. Do not consume more than you earn, and be sure that you know where your money goes. Do not buy everything that catches your fancy.

Now this does not mean that you should deprive yourself of the good things of life. Remember, God has given you all things richly to enjoy. In another place, God's Word boldly declares that prosperity and pleasures are the portion of those who obey and serve Him (see Job 36:11). So it is clear that God is not against your enjoying life's wonderful luxuries. However, what I am saying is that you should be moderate and considerate in your spending.

Most people who are materialistic are that way because they are insecure. They attach their worth to their possessions. They let the amount of money in their bank account dictate the way they feel or think about themselves.

But you need to understand, dear friend, that *your self-worth has nothing to do with your net worth!* Jesus said, *"One's life does not consist in the abundance of the things he possesses"* (Luke 12:15). This means that your life ... your self-worth ... is not defined by what you have. It is defined by who you are in Christ. Your real value as a person does not depend on your valuables. It is depends on the One whom you value. It depends on your relationship with God.

Money has to be respected as a very important tool in your hand if you desire godly prosperity. What you do not respect, you will not attract. The prodigal son disrespected money as a tool. He used it as a toy, wasting his resources when he should have wisely applied them. As a result, money drifted away from him, and he began to be in want.

3. THEY ARE FRIVOLOUS SPENDERS. THEY ARE NOT FRUGAL SAVERS.

Finally, poor money managers are frivolous spenders. The prodigal son "*spent all.*" The implication is that he saved nothing! He spent every single dollar that came into his hand. He did not put anything away. He had no investment whatsoever.

Bible-made millionaires understand that in order to increase wealth, you must never spend your money all at once. You must reserve part of your income for savings and investments. Millionaire Joseph was an expert at this. His wise saving habits preserved entire nations. His wise advise to Pharaoh is recorded in Genesis 41:34-36:

> *"Let Pharaoh do this, and let him appoint officers over the land, to collect one-fifth of the produce of the land of Egypt in the seven plentiful years.* **And let them gather all the food of those good years that are coming, and store up grain under the authority of Pharaoh, and let them keep food in the cities. Then that food shall be as a reserve for the land for the seven years of famine which shall be in the land of Egypt, that the land may not perish during the famine**" *(emphasis mine).*

Budget is a word that poor people hate to hear. But if you want to be a millionaire, you have to restrict your spending to a budget. You cannot afford to spend on impulse. Bible-made millionaires typically apportion their income into four parts. The first 10 percent of their income is designated as the Lord's tithe. I will speak more about this in the following chapter. Another 10 percent is apportioned for savings. Then yet another 10 percent is apportioned for investments, while the remaining 70 percent is designated for living expenses, including the payment of bills and so forth.

In today's world, there are many ways that you can save and invest your money. Countless options are available to you, and you can consult a good financial adviser for help. But whatever you do, do not spend all that you have. In the words of an African proverb, "*Do not eat with all your ten fingers!*"

You have seen from the classic example of the prodigal son that your ability to be wealthy is not primarily about how much you make. It depends largely on what you do with the money that you do make. You saw how he fell from grace to grass; from prosperity to the pig's pen. Though he received a rich inheritance from his father, because he lacked wisdom, he lost it all. A man who had once handled millions of dollars ended up in the pit. What could have been a source of income for a lifetime fizzled away in a very short time.

The Parable of the Prodigal Son still repeats itself today. There are many prodigals who, through foolish money management, are wasting their rich heritage. But this does not need to be the story of your life. Make up your mind to be a good, wise steward of the money that God gives you. When you show you can handle what you have got, you will be qualified to receive more.

MONEY MANAGEMENT AND TIME

> See then that you walk circumspectly, not as fools but as wise, redeeming the time, because the days are evil.
>
> Ephesians 5:15-16

> Walk in wisdom toward those who are outside, redeeming the time.
>
> Colossians 4:5

Benjamin Franklin, the first millionaire in American history, said, "*The way to wealth, if you desire it, is as plain as the way to market. It depends chiefly on two words,* industry *and* frugality. *Waste neither time nor money but make the best use of both.*"

It is not possible to talk about money management without mentioning the issue of time. Those who have no respect for time will also be lacking in their ability to manage money. You have heard it said before: Time is money. Therefore, the misuse of time equals the misuse of money.

Time slips through our hands like grains of sand in an hourglass, never to return again. Those who use time wisely are rewarded with riches, as well as productive and satisfying lives. Those who do not end up with a life full of regrets.

In Luke 19, the Lord Jesus told a very powerful parable that vividly illustrates this point. It is the Parable of the Ten Servants.

> He said therefore, A certain nobleman went into a far country to receive for himself a kingdom, and to return. And he called his ten servants, and delivered them ten pounds, and said unto them, Occupy till I come (verses 12-13, KJV).

One of the definitions of the word *occupy* is "to fill up time and space." So in essence, the nobleman was saying to his servants, *"Take the money that I am giving you and make the most of your time doing business with it."*

You cannot separate time from money. Bible-made millionaires understand this and as such make the most of their time. Those who while away their time, those who do not occupy, will end up being poor. Prosperous people, who make the most of their time doing business with everything that God has given them, will increase and become wealthy. In the parable, only those servants who "occupied" were rewarded with riches.

> "And so it was that when he returned, having received the kingdom, he then commanded these servants, to whom he had given the money, to be called to him, that he might know how much every man had gained by trading. Then came the first, saying, 'Master, your mina has earned ten minas.' And he said to him, 'Well done, good servant; because you were faithful in a very little, have authority over ten cities.' And the second came, saying, 'Master, your mina has earned five minas.' Likewise he said to him, 'You also be over five cities'" (verses 15-19).

However, the servant who squandered his time and resources suffered great loss.

> "Then another came, saying, 'Master, here is your mina, which I have kept put away in a handkerchief. For I feared you, because you are an austere man. You collect what you did not deposit, and reap what you did not sow.' And he said to him, 'Out of your own mouth I will judge you, you wicked servant. You knew that I was an austere man, collecting what I did not deposit and reaping what I did not sow. Why then did you not put my money in the bank, that at my coming I might have collected it with interest?' And he said to those who stood by, 'Take the mina from him, and give it to him who has ten minas.' (But they said to him, 'Master, he has ten minas.') For I say to you, that to everyone who has will be given; and from him who does not have, even what he has will be taken away from him" (verses 20-26).

If you desire to be a Bible-millionaire, you need to embrace the biblical philosophy of time management. Poverty is the product of poor time management, while prosperity is the product of good time management. I have never seen a poor man who was time- conscious. In the same regard, I have never met a rich man who had no regard for time.

Time is more than the clock or the calendar. Time is your very life! Benjamin Franklin also wisely said, "*Does thou love life, then do not squander time; for that is the stuff life is made of.*" Time is the hardest currency God has given you to trade with; it is meant to be redeemed wisely, not spent foolishly.

Major Time Wasters and How to Avoid Them

Bible-made millionaires guard their time jealously. They do not allow anything frivolous or unimportant to encroach upon their valuable time. Likewise, you must not allow anything or anyone to waste your time. Say "no" to any demand on your time that does not move you toward the fulfillment of your prosperous destiny.

I want to briefly mention common time wasters and how you can avoid them. Your ability to deal with them effectively will largely determine how successful you are in your career or business.

1. Needless Telephone Interruptions Or Conversations

Top on my list are unnecessary telephone interruptions. When the phone rings, it breaks your train of thought, interrupts you, and distracts you from what you were doing. By the time you hang up, you often find it hard to get back to the work in front of you.

How to avoid them: Assign a specific timeframe in which you will pick up calls. When you know you want to brainstorm or have some thinking time, turn off your ringer. An answering machine is a must for the Bible-made millionaire. Return calls at the time you have designated to receive or give phone calls.

2. Unexpected Or Unofficial Visitors

Socializing and idle conversations take up enormous amounts of valuable time. Unexpected or drop-in visitors can be extremely distracting. They drop by your office, distract you from your work, and impair your effectiveness.

They also talk endlessly about unimportant matters. It has been estimated that as much as 75 percent of time at work is spent interacting with other people. Unfortunately, half of this time is spent in idle chatter that has nothing to do with the work at hand.

How to avoid it: Have a strict no-visitor policy. Keep to the rule that anyone who comes to see you at work must be business-related. When you are known for this, your visitors will respect you and restrict personal visits only to your home. You must especially enforce this if you are a business owner. The rules that apply to your employees must also apply to you. No one is above the law!

3. PROCRASTINATION

You have probably heard it said: *Procrastination is the thief of time.* Indirectly it is also a thief of money. It is responsible for lost opportunities. People have lost contracts to competitors due to lack of action. Indecision and delay cost more time than most people realize. While there is a place for caution and careful deliberation, you must be careful not to overdo it. Strike when the iron is hot!

How to avoid it: Decision delayed is destiny denied. Do not overdrag issues that need to be addressed immediately. Place top priority on implementation. Give yourself deadlines. Financially successful people know how important it is to develop the ability to make up their minds quickly.

MAKING THE MOST OF YOUR TIME: WORK HARDER, WORK FASTER, WORK SMARTER!

These three phrases are my formula for success. Remember them, and you will occupy your time with purpose, leaving no room for trivialities.

- ✓ **Work harder:** Concentrate with greater intensity on your work. Discipline yourself to work without interruption, diversion, or distraction. There is no substitute for hard work in the school of success.
- ✓ **Work faster:** Develop a faster tempo in your work. Do not be sluggish. Proverbs 6:9-10 says, *How long will you slumber, O sluggard? When will you rise from your sleep? A little sleep, a little slumber, a little folding of the hands to sleep—so shall your poverty come on you like a prowler, and your need like an armed man.*

Sluggishness is one of the greatest deterrents to financial success. On the other hand, the combination of working hard and fast will get more done in a single day than most get done in a week. To be prosperous, you must work with enthusiasm and zeal, *not lagging in diligence, fervent in spirit* (Romans 12:11).

- ✓ **Work smarter:** Simplify your work by reducing the number of steps necessary to complete the tasks. Batch your tasks—do a series of similar jobs together. Do more important things first. These have a higher potential payoff. Do things that you are better at: Do things in which you naturally excel. This way you can get more done with a higher level of quality. Be meticulous. Make fewer mistakes—try to take time to do the job right the first time.

Invest Your Time. Do Not Spend It!

Bible-made millionaires treat time as they would money. So invest your time. Do not spend it frivolously. Have zero tolerance for time wasters. Riches are not possible without excellent time management. So master your time. Operate on a schedule. Have a set time for everything that you do.

Do not just do things as you feel. Apportion a specific time to accomplish specific tasks. Structure your life so that you are efficient and effective.

When you know how to handle your money wisely, you will never lament about your former days being better than today. No! Instead, your tomorrow will always be better and brighter than the day before. Like Millionaire Isaac, you will begin to prosper, and you will continue prospering until you become very prosperous (see Genesis 26:13)!

Chapter 9

Secret #7: Be a Sower

"While the earth remains, **Seedtime and harvest**, Cold and heat, Winter and summer, And day and night shall not cease."

Genesis 8:22, emphasis mine

There's no doubt about it: Every principle of biblical wealth that I have discussed in this book is extremely vital. However, your actually becoming a Bible-made millionaire will depend on this last, most important key—your ability to sow financial seeds.

You may love God with all your heart and be certain about your God-given purpose. You may have awesome plans and strategies with which to carry out your assignment. You may even be a person of integrity, strong and persistent in your faith. You may be the wisest money manager there is, but all these fine qualities will be in vain if you are not a sower.

A farmer may work his ground meticulously, he may fertilize it with the highest quality soil-enriching materials, he may get state-of-the-art machinery … yet if he leaves out the vital element of seed-sowing, he will not have a harvest. His nice-looking, well-tilled, richly fertilized ground will remain as bare and barren as ever … until he plants seeds into it.

This is so clear from Genesis 8:22: *You can only expect to reap a harvest if you have sown a seed.* No other quality or virtue can compensate for this. No matter how diligently a farmer attends to his farm, regardless of how skillful he is in the science of agriculture, if he refuses to plant a seed into the ground, he will never, ever reap a harvest. Seed-sowing is the only *bona fide* way by which anyone can reap a harvest. There is simply no way around it!

Financial seed-sowing, otherwise known as giving, is the primary means by which God has chosen to multiply wealth to His people. You cannot fast and pray your way into prosperity. You can only give your way to prosperity! Riches do not respond to fasting and praying; they respond to giving. Without seedtime, there cannot be harvest time. If you do not sow, you cannot reap. If you do not give, you cannot get. It is as simple as that!

Kingdom prosperity is a product of kingdom giving. Jesus said, "Give, and it will be given to you: **good measure**, **pressed down**, **shaken together**, and **running over** will be put into your bosom. For with the same measure that you use, it will be measured back to you" (Luke 6:38).

Note that Jesus did not say, "*Pray, and it will be given unto you.*" He said, "*Give.*" Now someone may ask, "*Well, didn't Jesus teach us in the Lord's Prayer to ask the Father for daily bread? Does this not mean that we should pray for money?*"

Let me first point out that the words *daily bread* refer to the things required for your daily sustenance. These are your most basic needs. But what Jesus was referring to in Luke 6:38 is much more than a mere daily ration. Take a look at the adjectives He uses: "*good measure, pressed down, shaken together, and running over.*" These are all images of superabundance and plenty. It describes much more than the supply of daily needs. It presents the picture of a continuous overflow of wealth—a lifetime of riches!

Jesus was not just talking about mere *sustenance*. He was talking about a mighty *surplus*! Friend, if you desire surplus, Jesus says to *give*. Prayer may produce your daily supply. But giving will command to you divine surplus. In short, *you should pray for daily bread but you should give for divine surplus*. The choice is yours: Do you want surplus or only a daily ration? Remember, surplus—more than enough and wealth—are your portion in the Lord. Do not settle for just enough. Choose to give your way to millionaire status!

RADICALLY CHANGE YOUR FINANCIAL STATUS BY SACRIFICIAL GIVING

Do you desperately need a financial miracle? Do you desire a radical change in your economic status? Then sow seeds as you never have before! Provoke your prosperity through the power of sacrificial giving.

Sacrificial giving takes place when you give out of your need. It is one thing to sow a seed when you can afford it; it is yet another to give when you barely have enough for your basic needs. Whenever you have a need, do not just give … give sacrificially. Sacrificial giving has an extra- special place in God's heart. It provokes Him to move on a person's behalf and to radically change their financial situation. This was what a little widow woman of Zarephath who lived in the Prophet Elijah's day discovered. Her story is found in 1 Kings 17.

> Then the word of the LORD came to him, saying, "Arise, go to Zarephath, which belongs to Sidon, and dwell there. See, I have commanded a widow there to provide for you." So he arose and went to Zarephath. And when he came to the gate of the city, indeed a widow was there gathering sticks. And he called to her and said, "Please bring me a little water in a cup, that I may drink." And as she was going to get it, he called to her and said, "Please bring me a morsel of bread in your hand." So she said, "As the LORD your God lives, I do not have bread, only a handful of flour in a bin, and a little oil in a jar; and see, I am gathering a couple of sticks that I may go in and prepare it for myself and my son, that we may eat it, and die." And Elijah said to her, "Do not fear; go and do as you have said, but make me a small cake from it first, and bring it to me; and afterward make some for yourself and your son. For thus says the LORD God of Israel: 'The bin of flour shall not be used up, nor shall the jar of oil run dry, until the day the LORD sends rain on the earth.'" So she went away and did according to the word of Elijah; and she and he and her household ate for many days. The

> bin of flour was not used up, nor did the jar of oil run dry, according to the word of the LORD which He spoke by Elijah (verses 8-16).

God knew how desperately this poor woman needed a financial breakthrough. She was down to her very last meal. As we would say today, she was down to her last penny. However, God did not command her to fast and pray. He commanded her to give. She barely had anything at all, yet God asked her to give up the little that she had. God told Elijah, "*I have commanded a widow there to provide for you.*"

How could God command someone who had barely anything to provide for His prophet? To the natural mind, this would seem ridiculous. But the ways of God are far different and superior to men. While the world says, "Get more and you will have more," God says, "Give more and you will get more."

In God's divine economy, the seed is one of the most powerful keys for financial release. Unless you are willing to let go of what is in your hand, God cannot let loose of what He has in His hand for you. This is why God commanded the widow to sow a seed in the time of her direst need. God wanted to end her problem. He wanted to change her status, and the surest way to do it was to get her to sow a sacrificial seed.

Sure enough, when, in obedience, she gave up what she had, her situation changed radically from that of poverty to prosperity. From that point on, her food and money supply was never used up: *The bin of flour was not used up, nor did the jar of oil run dry, according to the word of the LORD which He spoke by Elijah*. It never again ran dry. In one instant, her financial status changed dramatically. She went from *bankruptcy* to *buoyancy; from last meal* to *lifetime income!* This is what sacrificial giving will do for you.

Friend, giving is one of the surest ways by which you can promote yourself out of your current financial level to a higher one. Bible-made millionaires of old understood this principle, and as such, they were selfless givers. They did not withhold anything that they had from the Lord.

Millionaire Abraham stands out as one of the greatest givers of all time. He gave and gave and gave to God until he offered up his most beloved son. His sacrificial giving moved God to release an uncommon blessing upon him:

> Then the Angel of the LORD called to Abraham a second time out of heaven, and said: "By Myself I have sworn, says the LORD, because you have done this thing, and have not withheld your son, your only son—blessing I will bless you, and multiplying I will multiply your descendants as the stars of the heaven and as the sand which is on the seashore; and your descendants shall possess the gate of their enemies. In your seed all the nations of the earth shall be blessed, because you have obeyed My voice."
>
> Genesis 22:15-18

Millionaire David was also an outstanding giver. We discovered earlier on how Millionaire David gave $85 million worth of gold and $20 million worth of silver of his own personal money to the construction of the temple of the Lord (see 1 Chronicles 29:3-5, TLB). His sacrificial giving was mightily honored of the Lord, for David's glorious testimony at the end of his life was that *he died in a good old age, full of days and riches and honor* (1 Chronicles 29:28).

Millionaire Solomon powerfully followed his father's example of sacrificial giving. Solomon did not just give; he gave without limit. First Kings 8:5 says that he offered as gifts unto the Lord: *sheep and oxen that could not be counted or numbered for multitude.* His lavish giving provoked a great blessing upon his life, and in 1 Kings 9:1-5, God Himself personally appeared to him and pronounced a blessing upon him. The effect of this great blessing is clearly documented in the next chapter, 1 Kings 10:

> The weight of gold that came to Solomon yearly was six hundred and sixty-six talents of gold, besides that from the traveling merchants, from the income of traders, from all the kings of Arabia, and from the governors of the country. And King Solomon made two hundred large shields of hammered gold; six hundred shekels of gold went into each shield. He also made three hundred shields of hammered gold; three minas of gold went into each shield. The king put them in the House of the Forest of Lebanon. Moreover the king made a great throne of ivory, and overlaid it with pure gold. The throne had six steps, and the top of the throne was round at the back; there were armrests on either side of the place of the seat, and two lions stood beside the armrests. Twelve lions stood there, one on each side of the six steps; nothing like this had been made for any other kingdom. All King Solomon's drinking vessels were gold, and all the vessels of the House of the Forest of Lebanon were pure gold. Not one was silver, for this was accounted

> as nothing in the days of Solomon. For the king had merchant ships at sea with the fleet of Hiram. Once every three years the merchant ships came bringing gold, silver, ivory, apes, and monkeys. So King Solomon surpassed all the kings of the earth in riches and wisdom (verses 14-23).

Of a truth, the blessing of God will make you rich (see Proverbs 10:22). And your sacrificial giving is what will command God's wealth; producing blessings upon your life.

Stop praying and fasting for money … start giving! Godly prosperity does not answer to prayer or fasting; it answers to giving. Put your financial seeds in the ground, and you will reap a great harvest. When you have a need, do not just sow a seed; sow a sacrificial seed, and watch God work wonders on your behalf!

DO NOT EAT YOUR SEED!

> For as the rain comes down, and the snow from heaven, And do not return there, But water the earth, And make it bring forth and bud, That it may give **seed to the sower** And **bread to the eater**.
>
> Isaiah 55:10, emphasis mine

Many people have a problem with giving today because they lack understanding of one important truth: There are two parts to the income that God gives us: There is a seed part, and there is a bread part.

Stingy people who have a problem with giving fail to understand this key truth, and as a result, they withhold more than they should. They eat the seed part, instead of sowing it. They love to hold on tight to "their" money. They have sour faces when an offering is taken up in church. They think they are being talked out of giving "their" money.

First of all, never forget that the money in your hand is not yours. It is God's. Remember what Haggai 2:8 says, that all the silver and gold belongs to God. All of it! Sure, you worked and did your part, but if God had not blessed your efforts, your labor and hard work would have been in vain. Everything you have was *rained down* upon you from above. John 3:27 says, *"A man can receive nothing unless it has been given to him from heaven."*

And the God who blessed you with money says to not consume it all. Separate the bread from the seed. The bread is for eating, but the seed is for sowing. God gives us bread for consumption. This is money that we use to cover our basic needs, as well as other expenses. However, He also gives us seed. This is money that He intends for us to sow in order to reap a financial harvest. When you sow your seed, you will generate continuous wealth for yourself. Those who withhold and eat their seed are literally destroying their financial destiny.

> There is one who scatters, yet increases more;
> And there is one who withholds more than is right, But it leads to poverty.
>
> Proverbs 11:24

The seed is the primary way that God has designated to generate ongoing riches in your life. The fact of the matter is, if you stop giving, you will stop receiving. If you stop sowing, you will stop harvesting. Whenever money comes to your hand, carefully discern what portion of it is seed and what part is bread. Do not eat the seed, but sow it as God commands, and you will keep growing financially. The more you sow, the more you will reap.

> But this I say: He who sows sparingly will also reap sparingly, and he who sows bountifully will also reap bountifully. So let each one give as he purposes in his heart, not grudgingly or of necessity; for God loves a cheerful giver.
>
> 2 Corinthians 9:6-7

It is also important that you give willingly and wholeheartedly. Do not give grudgingly. Give in a spirit of appreciation, knowing that all you have comes from Him in the first place. Do not give as if you were doing God a favor.

Regardless of the economic conditions around you, keep on sowing. Give financial seeds even when you have a great financial need. Do not let an economic recession stop you from giving. You discovered from the case of the widow of Zarephath that the best time to give is in the time of need. Remember how God commanded Millionaire Isaac to keep sowing in the midst of famine. As he did, he prospered greatly.

Giving never reduces you. It only increases you. So give all that God commands with all your heart. Do not give one cent less than what He impresses upon your heart. Also, do not procrastinate. Do not delay in giving what you promised the Lord. The sooner you get your seed into the ground, the quicker you will receive your harvest.

> When you make a vow to God, do not delay to pay it; For He has no pleasure in fools. Pay what you have vowed.
>
> Ecclesiastes 5:4

> "When you make a vow to the LORD your God, you shall not delay to pay it; for the LORD your God will surely require it of you, and it would be sin to you."
>
> Deuteronomy 23:21

When you understand how much you stand to gain by giving, you will not have a *sour face* when an offering is being taken. No. You will have a *smiling face!* You will rejoice and dance before the Lord with all your heart because you know that the seed that leaves your hands does not leave your life. It goes into your future to prepare a great financial harvest for you!

Types of Giving

There are various types of giving that God has commanded in His Word. Top on the list is the tithe.

1. The Tithe

The word *tithe* means "the tenth part." But not just any tenth part. Your tithe specifically refers to *the first tenth part.* The tithe is the first 10 percent of your income, specifically designated by God as the holy portion belonging to Him alone. It is holy and must be set apart, reserved exclusively for Him.

> "And all the tithe of the land, whether of the seed of the land or of the fruit of the tree, is the LORD's. It is holy to the LORD... And concerning the tithe of the herd or the flock, of whatever passes under the rod, the tenth one shall be holy to the LORD."
>
> Leviticus 27:30, 32

It is the covenant privilege and responsibility of every believer to worshipfully offer unto the Lord the first tenth part of their income. Do not pay your tithe after you have written out the checks for your bills. This does not honor God. Your tithe must come first. God is a God of order. To enjoy the fullness of His blessings, you must do things exactly as He has commanded.

To default on the tithe is to rob God. Failure to pay it incurs a curse from the Lord, which, in turn, opens the door to the devourer.

> "Will a man rob God? Yet you have robbed Me! But you say, 'In what way have we robbed You?' In tithes and offerings. You are cursed with a curse, For you have robbed Me,
> Even this whole nation. Bring all the tithes into the storehouse, That there may be food in My house, And try Me now in this," Says the LORD of hosts, "If I will not open for you the windows of heaven And pour out for you such blessing That there will not be room enough to receive it.

> "And I will rebuke the devourer for your sakes, So that he will not destroy the fruit of your ground, Nor shall the vine fail to bear fruit for you in the field," Says the LORD of hosts; "And all nations will call you blessed, For you will be a delightful land," Says the LORD of hosts.
>
> Malachi 3:8-12

If you want to enjoy financial blessings, you must be a consistent tither. Faithfully bring your tithes into God's house, your home church, where you are spiritually nurtured and cared for.

J. D. Rockefeller, the great American billionaire and a devout Northern Baptist, was said to have faithfully paid his tithe to his church right from his very first paycheck. And the more he gave, the more prosperous he became. The Rockefeller family went on to become one of the richest and most philanthropic families in the United States!

When you pay your tithes as God commands, things will never be tight for you! The windows of heaven will always be open to you, and you will enjoy a steady flow of God's blessings in your life.

For businesspeople or those who work on commission, your tithe would constitute the first tenth of your profits or increase.

> "You shall truly **tithe all the increase** of your grain that the field produces year by year."
>
> Deuteronomy 14:22, emphasis mine

In practical terms, suppose your company's expenditure for the month was $25,000, and your income was $30,000. The difference, which is $5,000, would constitute your profit. This is what you should tithe off of. So in this case, your corporate tithe would be $500. As you tithe your corporate profits, you will discover that your business will never, ever go down. While others are folding up, yours will be rising up. This is a truth that has been proven true in the lives of several entrepreneurs who attend Dominion International Center.

Your tithe authorizes God to become an enemy to your enemies. You are then able to build a great financial future with no resistance from hell. Your tithe creates protection, financial abundance, and all other miracles you desire in your life. Tithing guarantees you favor with God. Friend, tithe faithfully, and you will see financial miracles take place. Abraham, the prosperous father of faith, paid tithes as God commanded and prospered as a result (Genesis 14:17-20). You are a seed of Abraham, so do the works of Abraham, and you will enjoy his blessings.

2. WORSHIP OFFERINGS

As a covenant child of God, you are mandated to never appear before God empty. Worship God with an offering every time you come into His presence.

> Give to the LORD the glory due His name;
> Bring an offering, and come into His courts.
> Oh, worship the LORD in the beauty of holiness!
> Tremble before Him, all the earth.
>
> Psalm 96:8-9

> "Three times a year all your males shall appear before the LORD your God in the place which He chooses.... They shall not appear before the LORD empty-handed. Every man shall give as he is able, according to the blessing of the LORD your God which He has given you."
>
> Deuteronomy 16:16-17

Unlike the tithe, there is no designated amount that you are required to give as a worship offering to the Lord. You should give out of your free will as you have been blessed of God.

> So let each one give as he purposes in his heart, not grudgingly or of necessity; for God loves a cheerful giver.
>
> 2 Corinthians 9:7

However, remember that whatever you give to God must be given with thought and honor. Giving from the heart commands blessings from God.

3. Giving to the Poor

Bible-made millionaires have a propensity to charitable deeds. Millionaire Job, who was the richest man during his time, said:

> "Because I delivered the poor who cried out, The fatherless and the one who had no helper. The blessing of a perishing man came upon me, And I caused the widow's heart to sing for joy. I put on righteousness, and it clothed me;

> My justice was like a robe and a turban. I was eyes to the blind, And I was feet to the lame. I was a father to the poor,
> And I searched out the case that I did not know. I broke the fangs of the wicked, And plucked the victim from his teeth."
>
> Job 29:12-17

The ministry of our Lord Jesus gave generously to the poor. He was always preaching about giving to the poor. He told the rich young ruler that the key to having eternal treasures was giving to the poor.

> So when Jesus heard these things, He said to him, "You still lack one thing. Sell all that you have and distribute to the poor, and you will have treasure in heaven; and come, follow Me."
>
> Luke 18:22

> Let him who stole steal no longer, but rather let him labor, working with his hands what is good, that he may have something to give him who has need.
>
> Ephesians 4:28

God will abundantly bless you when you look upon the poor with compassion and favor them. Proverbs 22:9 says, *He who has a generous eye will be blessed, for he gives of his bread to the poor.*

As a matter of fact, did you know that any time you give to the poor, you are actually lending unto the Lord?

> He who has pity on the poor **lends** to the LORD,
> And He will pay back what he has given.
>
> Proverbs 19:17, emphasis mine

God is a God of integrity. He will not be indebted to any man. So you can be sure that He will reward your generosity big time. He will pay you back with interest!

4. Giving to the Saints/Fellow Believers

Not only should you sow financial seeds to the poor, you should also give to fellow believers. Galatians 6:10 says, *Therefore, as we have opportunity, let us do good to all, especially to those who are of the household of faith.*

There are great rewards for giving to your brothers and sisters in Christ.

> "And whoever gives one of these little ones only a cup of cold water in the name of a disciple, assuredly, I say to you, he shall by no means lose his reward."
>
> Matthew 10:42

When you create wealth for others, you will become wealthy yourself. Dr. Mike Murdock, my mentor and one of the wisest men I have ever known, once said, "What you make happen for others, God will make happen for you." This is so true. When you give to others, much more will come back to you.

Millionaire Mordecai was wealthy because he sought the wealth and well-being of his fellow Israelites. He did not just look out for himself.

> Now all the acts of his power and his might, and the account of the greatness of Mordecai, to which the king advanced him, are they not written in the book of the chronicles of the kings of Media and Persia? For Mordecai the Jew was second to King Ahasuerus, and was great among the Jews and well received by the multitude of his brethren, seeking the good of his people and speaking peace to all his countrymen.
>
> Esther 10:2-3.

One of the reasons why Millionaire Daniel increasingly became prosperous was because he strived to improve the lives of his brethren. He did not just look out for himself. As a result, he was elevated to a position of influence and affluence.

> Then the king promoted Daniel and gave him many great gifts; and he made him ruler over the whole province of Babylon, and chief administrator over all the wise men of Babylon. Also Daniel petitioned the king, and he set Shadrach, Meshach, and Abed-Nego over the affairs of the province of Babylon; but Daniel sat in the gate of the king.
>
> Daniel 2:48-49

When you seek the lifting of others, you yourself will be lifted. In your quest to wealth and success, share secrets with others along the way. Do not just seek wealth for yourself. Delight in the prosperity of others like you.

5. Giving to the Prophet

> Let him who is taught the word share in all good things with him who teaches.
>
> Galatians 6:6

There are also enormous financial blessings that will flow to you when you sow into the lives of anointed men and women of God. Such giving is greatly rewarded by the Lord. Jesus said, "*He who receives a prophet in the name of a prophet shall receive a prophet's reward. And he who receives a righteous man in the name of a righteous man shall receive a righteous man's reward*" (Matthew 10:41).

You are obligated by God to sow financial seeds into the lives of those who minister to you spiritually.

> If we have sown [the seed of] spiritual good among you, [is it too] much if we reap from your material benefits?
>
> 1 Corinthians 9:11, AMP

Most especially, it is your duty to financially honor your spiritual parents, who nurture and care for you on a regular basis. Never take your pastor's labor of love over you for granted.

> Let the elders who rule well be counted worthy of double honor, especially those who labor in the word and doctrine. For the Scripture says, "You shall not muzzle an ox while it treads out the grain," and, "The laborer is worthy of his wages."
>
> 1 Timothy 5:17-18

Some people will fuss over guest ministers who pay occasional visits to their church. They are quick to shower them with gifts, yet they have never once blessed their own pastor, who daily serves and ministers to them. This is absurd and meaningless.

While it is proper to sow financial gifts to visiting evangelists, apostles, evangelists, and so forth, the Bible clearly states that you should highly honor and celebrate your own ministers. On a regular basis, as God blesses you, sow into the lives of your spiritual parents. As you honor the special men and women that God has placed in your life, God will honor you, too.

6. GIVING TO YOUR NATURAL PARENTS

> "**Honor** your father and your mother, that your days may be long upon the land which the LORD your God is giving you."
>
> Exodus 20:12, emphasis mine

> "For God commanded, saying, 'Honor your father and your mother'; and, 'He who curses father or mother, let him be put to death.' But you say, 'Whoever says to his father or mother, "Whatever profit you might have received from me is a gift to God"—then he need not honor his father or mother.' Thus you have made the commandment of God of no effect by your tradition."
>
> Matthew 15:4-6

If you desire to live a long and prosperous life, you need to honor your earthly parents with financial gifts. Sowing financial seeds to your natural parents is a covenant key that unlocks a glorious financial destiny. Regardless of whether they are wealthier than you or not, you need to bless your parents with monetary gifts on a regular basis. Great blessings are released when a child blesses his parents.

Millionaire Jacob prospered as a result of his father's blessing, which he received after he offered his father a sumptuous meal.

> And he said, Bring it near to me, and I will eat of my son's venison, that my soul may bless thee. And he brought it near to him, and he did eat: and he brought him wine, and he drank. And his father Isaac said unto him, Come near now, and kiss me, my son. And he came near, and kissed him: and he smelled the smell of his raiment, and blessed him, and said, See, the smell of my son is as the smell of a field which the LORD hath blessed: Therefore God give thee of the dew of heaven, and the fatness of the earth, and plenty of corn and wine: Let people serve thee, and nations bow down to thee: be lord over thy brethren, and let thy mother's sons bow down to thee: cursed be every one that curseth thee, and blessed be he that blesseth thee.
>
> Genesis 27:25-29, KJV

Millionaire David also took good care of his parents (see 1 Samuel 22:1-4). There are many believers who treat their parents shabbily and yet expect to be blessed by God. It cannot happen. If you breach God's command to honor your parents, you cannot be honored or blessed by Him.

7. GIVING TO KINGDOM PROJECTS

As I mentioned earlier on, you are obligated to give toward the work of the expansion of God's kingdom. Money is needed to accomplish every ministry, vision, or project that has been commanded by the Lord.

As such, you should give generously to kingdom-advancing initiatives. These include church-building projects, missions, outreach efforts, and so forth. God commanded the Israelites to give for the building of His tabernacle.

> And Moses spoke to all the congregation of the children of Israel, saying, "This is the thing which the LORD commanded, saying: '**Take from among you an offering to the LORD. Whoever is of a willing heart, let him bring it as an offering to the LORD: gold, silver, and bronze**.' Then everyone came whose heart was stirred, and everyone whose spirit was willing, and they brought the LORD's offering for the work of the tabernacle of meeting, for all its service, and for the holy garments. The children of Israel brought a freewill offering to the LORD, all the men and women whose hearts were willing to bring material for all kinds of work which the LORD, by the hand of Moses, had commanded to be done.
>
> Exodus 35:4-5, 21, 29, emphasis mine

You cannot afford to be stingy if you want to be wealthy. The only way to sustain and multiply riches is through giving. It is absolutely impossible for you to become a Bible-made millionaire if you are stingy. The way God prospers is different from the way the world prospers. Worldly prosperity is based on how much you can get. The world says, *the more you can accumulate, the more you will have*. But godly prosperity is based on how much you can give. God says, *the more you give, the more you will get*. As a Bible-made millionaire, your prosperity is not a function of your *getting power*. It is function of your *giving power!*

Part 3

Come into Your Wealthy Place!

We went through fire and through water: but thou broughtest us out into a wealthy place.

Psalm 66:12b KJV

PUT THE PAST BEHIND YOU. GOD IS ABOUT TO DO SOMETHING *NEW* IN YOUR LIFE!

> "Do not remember the former things, Nor consider the things of old. Behold, I will do a new thing, Now it shall spring forth; Shall you not know it? I will even make a road in the wilderness And rivers in the desert."
>
> Isaiah 43:18-19

No matter where you are today financially, regardless of what you have gone through in times past, I declare unto you in the name of Jesus Christ our Lord: God is about to do something new for you!

Are you ready to join the millionaire's club?

Are you ready to change your financial status?

Then, dear friend, forget the former things. Do not brood over yesterday's setbacks because you are about to experience a *major comeback!*

You may have lost many things, *but God is the reason why you have not lost everything.*

You may have gone through a heartbreaking bankruptcy. You may have had to close your business down. You may have lost your house to foreclosure. Your car may have been repossessed. You may have just been laid off. Your bank account may be in the red. Yes, precious one, *you may have gone through hell and high water, but God is about to bring you into your wealthy place!*

It is a place that God has prepared for you to live in this life. It is a good and large land … a land flowing with milk and honey (Exodus 3:8) … a place where lack and poverty are totally non-existent, where you are out of debt, where your needs are met, and where you have plenty left over to be a blessing to others.

Yesterday's losses do not matter anymore. Today is what counts. Life may have dealt you a hard and bitter blow. You may have suffered setback upon setback. But *today* you can change it all. *You can break free from every cycle of poverty and limitation.*

If you would immediately get to work with the secrets I have shared in this book, your financial status will change for the best.

Remember, covenant wealth is not a matter of chance; it is a matter of covenant. The wealthy place is not only for a reserved few. It is for you!

God cares about you and has decreed that the time of your liberation and promotion is *now*. So do not settle for lower class; do not even accept middle-class status. You are destined to be in the upper class, to be above only and never beneath.

Someone may ask, "If everyone is in the upper class, then who will be the servants?" I say, "Whoever chooses to!" But if you embrace what I have shared, you will never be a slave to poverty or mediocrity. You will come into the wealthy place that God has prepared for you.

The wealthy place has nothing to do with geographical location. A person can live in a nation as prosperous as America and still live in a state of poverty. Yet another may live in a poor country and be wealthy.

The wealthy place has everything to do with your heavenly citizenship. You are a citizen of heaven, and you are entitled to a heavenly lifestyle. It is God's will that your days on earth be like the days of heaven ahead of you. Poverty is not your portion. Prosperity is!

No son of God is destined to be poor. No! We all have a rich heritage in the Lord. All those who are of faith are blessed with Abraham's blessings. As far as He is concerned, no son or daughter of His belongs to the lower class. You should not even settle for middle class. There is only one class that God has reserved for you to be in: the upper class. You are destined to be above only, never beneath!

Make up your mind to practice the biblical principles for covenant wealth that I have shared in this book.

Seek God's kingdom and His righteousness.

Lay hold of your God-given assignment and begin to run with your vision, using every divine strategy at your disposal.

Strive to be a person of integrity. Do not just make money. Work hard at maintaining a good reputation.

Persist in the face of all odds and handle whatever money God gives you with wisdom and prudence.

Above all, sow generously and gladly as God commands, watering your seeds with praise and expectation. Do all these things, and you cannot escape it: YOU WILL BECOME THE NEXT BIBLE-MADE MILLIONAIRE!

To order additional copies of

SEVEN SECRETS OF

BIBLE-MADE MILLIONAIRES

have your credit card ready and call
1 800-917-BOOK (2665)
1-866-370-6352

or e-mail
orders@selahbooks.com
info@dominioninternationalcenter.org

or order online at
www.selahbooks.com
www.dominionlifestyle.org

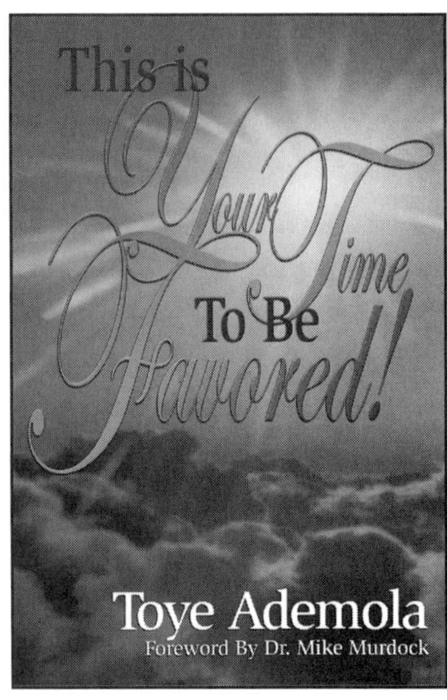

This is Your Time To Be Favored!

Price: $5.00
ISBN: 1-55306-158-6

Description: Although God does not discriminate amongst His people, one thing will always distinguish one person from another - the Favor of God! Discover how you can experience the uncommon release of God's blessings in your life. Discover how you can live above the average - This is your time to be favored!

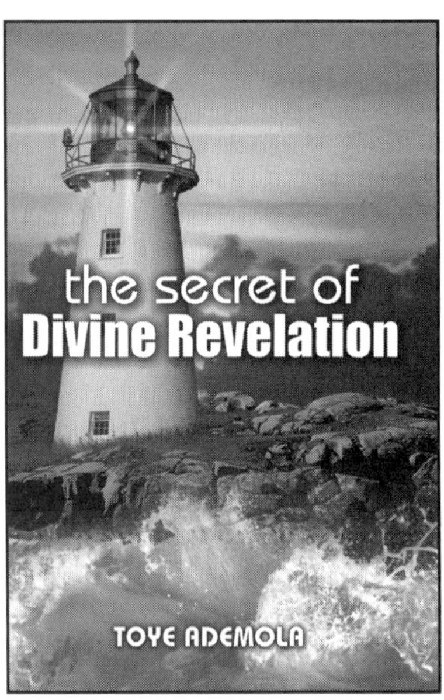

The Secret of Divine Revelation

Price: $5.00
ISBN: 1-55306-346-5

Description: God's Word is a rich gold mine. You need divine insight to locate and enjoy the abundant treasures and blessings of the word. The Secret of Divine Revelation will show you how you can gain access into God's divine mysteries. This revelation will bring a great revolution in your life. You will not be the same!

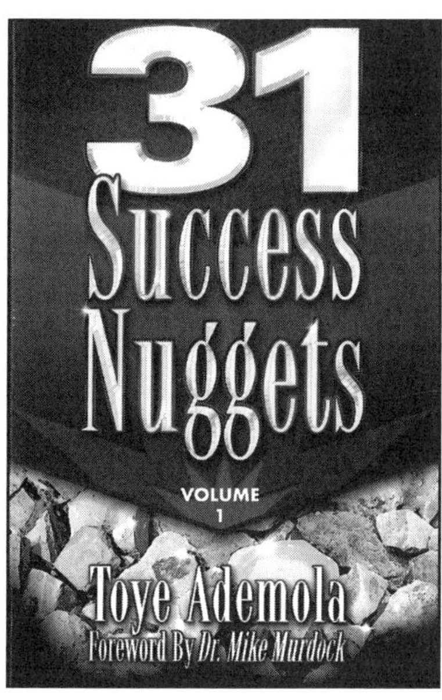

31 Success Nuggets

Price: $5
ISBN: 1-56394-162-7
Description: God has made super abundant provision to guarantee that you succeed in life. However, it is entirely up to you to make the move to become truly successful. In this devotional, Pastor Toye shares 31 Success Nuggets that reveal what you must do to experience outstanding success in every facet of your life. If you are tired of a life of mediocrity; if you have a passion for excellence, you must read this book!

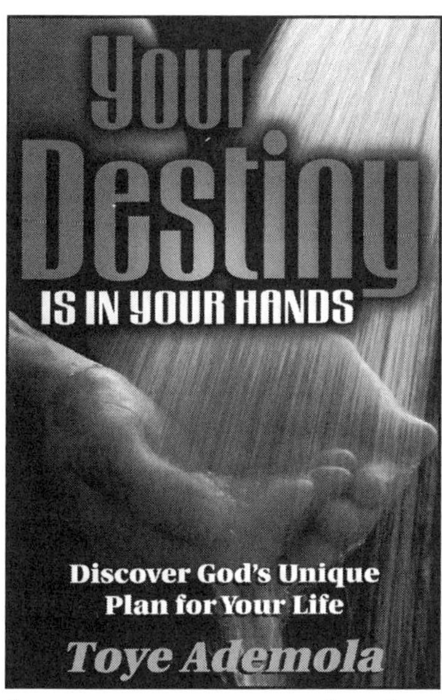

Your Destiny Is In Your Hands

Price: $10
ISBN: 1-56043-213-6

Description: You are divinely designed! God has a unique plan for you - a destiny set - in place before your birth. Your destiny is in your hands will lead you on the path to discover God's special plan for you. Toye Ademola demonstrates principles designed to equip you with wisdom and determination. You will begin to experience your great destiny as only God intended it!

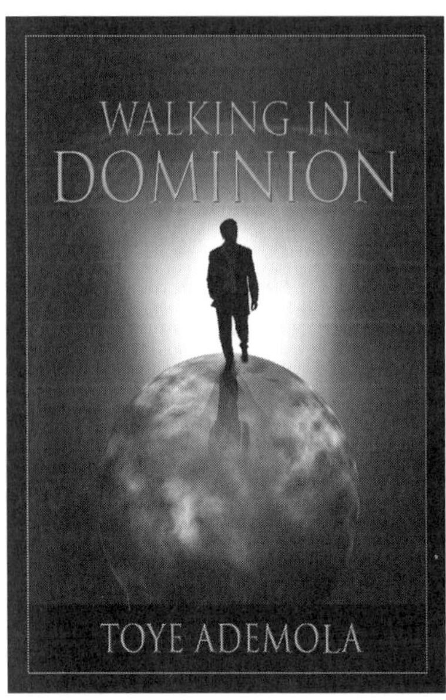

Walking In Dominion

Price: $15.99
ISBN: 978-1-58930-168-9
Description: You do not ever have to experience a 'down day' again! In *Walking In Dominion* you will learn how you can consistently live in victory every single day of your life! Your Savior and Lord paid the price for your redemption in FULL. Do not accept anything less than what He paid for! Do not accept the world's woes. God has made you a winner. Do not let the storms of life subdue you…you are destined to be above only, never beneath. You are made for mastery, not for misery. You are a victor, not a victim!

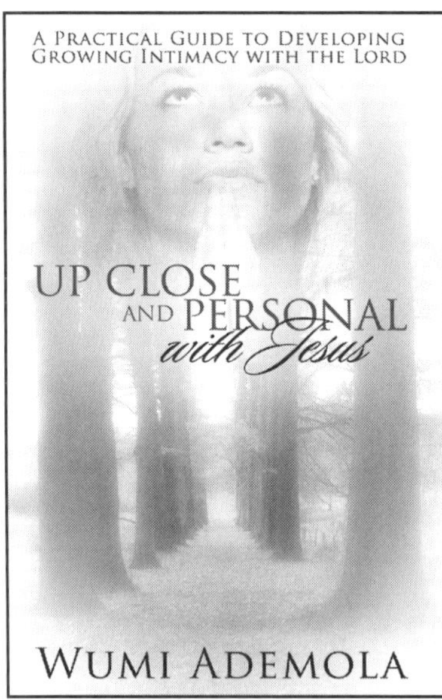

Up-Close & Personal With Jesus

Price: $10.99
ISBN: 978-1-58930-168-9
Description: Does your heart yearn to know the Lord in a real and intimate way? Then let Up-Close & Personal with Jesus show you how! This book will take you through a practical step by step guide of what you must do to develop a strong and vibrant relationship with the Lord. Each chapter ends with simple action steps that you can take and immediately start enjoying a level of closeness with Him that you had never known before.